TAKING
CALCULATED
RISKS

TAKING CALCULATED RISKS

THE RISE OF RAMESH BHATIA, TITAN OF INDUSTRY

RAMESH BHATIA

President and CEO, ATCO Rubber Products, Inc.

Acknowledgments

~

I *would like to thank* Mr. Marvin B. Gardner, who gave me the first opportunity to make a living, expanded my engineering knowledge, and started me on my path to success. To Mr. Ed Moyer, who defied his superiors and took a chance on me. To Kamal Ladha, who believed in my talents and offered me the fortuitous opportunity to enter the new and unproven industry of flexible ducts. To the entire ATCO team, who stood by me in good times and bad—you all helped take our company to new heights year after year. I am eternally grateful for your trust in me. And most of all, a special thanks to Mr. Charles B. Anderson, who gave me his unwavering support, led me on the right path in the duct business, and fostered skills within me that I never knew I had.

I would also like to thank my father and mother, who instilled good values in me while I was growing up and who demonstrated how loving a married couple can be. To my wife, Kalpana Bhatia, who stood by me in many challenging times and who was my best advisor—you had full faith in my ability to be successful in whatever I did.

To my dear brother, Harendra, who has been my friend all our lives but who opened my eyes to many new opportunities on a personal and professional level, and worked hard to make me fulfill my dreams.

AND

My two children, Anita and Niraj, who suffered through many lonely evenings when I was away from home traveling or meeting business associates. I missed many important events where I should have been present.

Forty Years of Lessons Learned

1. Show you are human—reveal your weaknesses.
2. Dare to be different—differentiate yourself through imagination, expertise, and risk-taking nature.
3. Take responsibility for decisions—wrong or right.
4. Always include your team as your partners—say "we" and not "I."
5. Develop a passion to work for reasons that go beyond money and status.
6. Understand the emotional makeup of other people and treat them accordingly.
7. Gratitude is the most exquisite form of courtesy.
8. Trust yourself; it will allow you to live with your decisions all your life.
9. If you cannot love yourself, you cannot love another person.
10. A goal without a plan is just a wish.
11. Rendering quality customer service is both a responsibility and an opportunity.
12. Ignoring what customers want is the biggest mistake.
13. Be humble and never let arrogance take over, irrespective of what you achieve.
14. In business, be nimble and be ready to take risks if that's what the market demands.
15. Have affirmative thoughts all the time, for they help you succeed.
16. The most important characteristics are honesty, competence, foresight, intelligence, and courageousness.

Table of Contents

~

Chapter 1

When *I was young,* I lived in the city of Patna. It was loud and hot. Rickshaws and street peddlers clamored in the dust. Crowds of Biharis bustled past small shopfronts with no sense of order, weaving in and out of the street as buggy drivers shooed them away like farm animals. Sometimes, I'd marvel at an automobile honking its way through the throng. Cars were rare in the '40s in India—most arrived by boat from Britain. That long and expensive trek made them status symbols of that rare Bihari who left our country and became wealthy, successful, and modern. To keep up with all the traffic, city officials installed stoplights at busy intersections, but the blinking lights failed to calm the chaos. Instead, they hung as bright and useless as a piece of jewelry above the crowd.

I remember walking these streets with my brother Harendra and feeling utterly lost in the commotion. I was six, and the city felt strange to me, like I didn't quite belong. It was always a relief to turn my back to the bike horns and desperate cries of women selling household goods in the shade of tamarind trees and re-enter my house. Closing the great wooden door behind me, the street noise hushed. I relished the silence before it was filled with another kind of noise—the shouts and cries and pan-clacking of an Indian family of ten.

My father, Lajpat Rai Bhatia, ran the household as best he could. He was a well-built, energetic man whose face was kind, but the creases around his eyes reflected the strain of hustling to make ends meet for his wife and eight children. My mother, Shakuntala, was a beautiful woman with soft, smooth skin. I remember her in the kitchen making meals or rushing out the door to haggle with the produce vendors down the street. We were middle class, but with so many mouths to feed, my parents were constantly worried about getting food on the table.

Sometimes, my mother would come home and we'd ask, "*Bhabhiji*, what are we eating tonight?"

"Reach in my pocket," she'd say, "and if there's money, we'll eat well. If not, we'll find a way. We always find a way."

Luckily, my father was well trained to care for a family of this size. He himself was the eldest of seven and, as is customary in Indian culture, was responsible for caring for his six younger brothers and sisters growing up. He was born and reared in Sialkot, an industrious suburb of the city of Lahore in the Punjab region of what is now Pakistan. Back then, it was still a part of India. His father, Anant Ram Bhatia, was the headmaster of a public school. This was a prestigious position in the late 1800s, and my grandfather earned that distinction because of his sincerity and integrity. There was no public transportation back then, and I heard stories about how he walked to and from school every day like clockwork, even though it was a trek of several miles. I imagine the neighbors could tell the exact time of day by seeing him pass—that is how principled he was.

As soon as my father was old enough, he began to work and help increase the household income. Sialkot was—and still is—known as a hub for high-quality wood and leather goods. The city became famous all over India for its sporting equipment, such as tennis and badminton rackets, field hockey sticks, and cricket bats. The British would send their broken sports items to Sialkot for repair, and entrepreneurs started businesses to produce goods for India's obsession with sport. My father jumped into the local fray as a teenager by borrowing money from family friends. He quickly built a reputation like his father's—he was honest and respected, and these qualities made him one of the most successful businessmen in Punjab. With his good looks and disarming smile, he traveled all over India and made enough money to build a beautiful home for himself and his family, including all of his siblings. He didn't mind the travel—India was rapidly changing in the '20s and '30s, and he loved meeting people from different corners of the country—but he was always happy to return home. He loved Sialkot and didn't once think of living anywhere else.

One of his regular business trips was to Patna, the capital city of Bihar state, where a British regiment was stationed. Patna was a bustling city on the banks of the Ganges River. In fact, it's one of the oldest continuously inhabited places in the world. For over 2,500 years, the city has passed from Gupta kings to Mughal emperors, and under each ruler, no matter their religion or ethnicity, Patna thrived as a mercantile city—a crossroads of international trade and culture. Wanting to take advantage of this, the British opened a factory here in 1620, and other European nations came in droves to make their own trade posts in the lucrative market. In the mid-1700s, the East India Company took control of the region and set up a British Raj, effectively giving rule over India to the British Empire. Over time, the British built several universities, such as Patna College, Patna Science College, Bihar College of Engineering, and the Prince of Wales Medical College. The city became famous as the cradle of education in India, and soon other British and American institutions followed with their own schools and English programs for locals and foreigners alike.

Those institutions in turn opened up a large market for sporting goods. My father provided them with his usual array of high-quality equipment, and soon he was in high demand. His British customers loved working with him, and as they chatted over new orders for cricket bats, my father would complain about the arduous 1,300-kilometer journey back and forth between Sialkot and Patna. He'd lightheartedly grumble about the slow trains—"Slow," the officers would joke, "if they show up at all!"—and they'd protest whenever my father had to leave again.

"Get a house here in Patna," they told him. "Wouldn't it be so much nicer if your family lived here? We're most of your business anyway. Plus, your brothers and sisters could get a top-notch education here. We know the admissions people at the universities, you know . . ."

My father never wanted to move away from Sialkot, but on the train ride back that evening, he began to think about the possibility. Patna's schools were unmatched, and the officers weren't lying when they praised his robust business status in town. Back home, he discussed the possibility with my mother, and in 1942 decided to make the move. The entire Bhatia clan, led by Lajpat Rai Bhatia, started a new life in a new city in a new state in what would soon become a new fractured and devastated country.

———•———

Chapter 2

~

I *was born two years later in 1944.* My aunts and uncles traveled from Sialkot to bless my birth—later on, I was told it was quite auspicious for my elders to travel so far to welcome me into the world, seeing that I was the youngest of so many children. But they came, and our little house on the alley was filled with celebration and laughter for months. Looking into the windows of my house, you wouldn't guess a war was raging across the globe. It was as if my family focused on me as a little ball of joy to distract them from the dark times overheard on the news and felt in the air in the city streets.

World War II had started five years before I was born, and for the first few years it was merely a European war, fought far from Patna. However, by the time I arrived in my parents' arms, the war had stretched to India's doorstep, and Patna became a major logistical hub for British forces. That year, my father was hired by his British colleagues to manage the British Army Distribution Center in Dinapur, a neighborhood at the western edge of Patna. These officers had known my father for years and trusted him entirely—even though he had zero experience in that line of work.

Like all things, he learned the role quickly and threw himself into it with a passion for high standards inherited from his father. My father would start work at 8 a.m. and labor deep into the night. The meticulous care he took in his sporting business he now channeled with even greater intensity into this new position. He was entrusted by the British with an important job—one that felt vital to the success of the British and Indian forces against the Axis of Evil—and he knew that, no matter how trivial or small his job duties may have been, they were to be done with the utmost integrity. One of my earliest memories was of him surprising us kids with a handful of British-made goodies—crumbly biscuits and milk chocolates—which we gobbled up like little pigs. The next night, my siblings and I mobbed him, pawing at his pockets to see if he'd brought more treats home.

"Did you bring chocolates today?" my older brother asked.

"Yes, Daddy, did you? Did you?" my sisters and brothers chimed in.

"No, my children," he said, his voice tired but warm. We were crestfallen, and one of my brothers began to whine. My father shushed him and kneeled down, waving his hands for us to gather closer to him. "Now listen to me; I bought those chocolates yesterday for you as a treat. Today, I didn't have enough money to buy more."

"But they were so yummy," my sister said.

"I know. But if I took chocolates today and didn't pay for them, I would be cheating my employers." We understood, but our faces still showed the disappointment of having no biscuits that afternoon. He smiled at us. "Don't worry," he said. "There will be more money soon, and more treats in your future. But always remember this: We Bhatias don't steal."

This early lesson in business integrity left a deep impression on me. I grew up wanting more than my parents could provide, but they always worked as a team, and I always received what I needed. They never lied or stole or cheated. (Unless, of course, we were sitting down to a card game of Rummy—then all bets were off!) When it came to business and friendships, my parents believed in always being fair and equitable.

Their high ethical standard was matched by an equally impressive generosity. I was too young to understand what was going on at the time, but I remember my house filled with people I didn't know. Even after my aunts and uncles left, my parents would bring home adults, sometimes with their children, whose haggard faces lit up once they crossed our threshold and sat down exhausted in our living room chairs. My mother would cook huge meals, and my father would sit with them late into the night to talk in hushed voices about things I didn't understand—things like "partition" and "refugees" and "slaughter." I remember my father telling an old neighbor of his that "they" had taken his house and land in Sialkot. "I'm lucky," he said with a shake of his head, "that I moved my family here when we did. Who knows what would have happened if we'd stayed?" Then, the conversation would turn to politics, and I'd slide easily into sleep on the smooth concrete floor.

With all the hustle and hubbub in the house, I'd often escape into the alley to play with my friends. One of my best friends was an old man named Hira Lal—"Red Diamonds," as my children would later call him—who owned a wood factory behind our home. He had a big house on the alley with a large, airy backyard tucked away from the street noise of Patna. I loved to run and play games in that yard. He'd sit under a great old neem tree and smile as I ran myself ragged. Gulping for air, I'd stand next to him as he fished into his pockets to give me a treat. Sometimes it was a lollipop, other times a British chocolate—the

same brand my father would sometimes bring home when I was a toddler. Hira Lal was like a second father to me, and I adored his attention—especially since I didn't have to share it with my older siblings!

On one particularly hot night, he called me over. As I jumped from
foot to foot, salivating over what candy he'd pull out, Hira Lal said,
"Ramesh, tell me. What do you want to be when you grow up?"

I thought about his question but hesitated, not sure what to say. When
I grew up? When I was big and tall like he was?

"I'll give you your treat if you tell me," he said.

Energized, I replied with the first thought that came into my head:
"I want to move away from India and become big and famous!"

He let out a startled laugh and reached into his pocket to fish out
a candy. Something in his eyes made me feel like he understood what
I had blurted out to him in that dusty yard, even though I didn't fully
get it myself.

But as I got older, this desire only deepened. I always knew I wanted
to leave, travel the world, see new cities, meet new people, and explore
as much as this planet could offer. Patna was old and hot and dirty and
noisy. Even as a kid, it felt small and stuck in its ways. As the strangers
in my house would tell tales of their homes and families in Sialkot, I
too wanted to visit distant lands. Most children feel this way—wanting
to leave what they've always known to search for themselves elsewhere.
As small as I was, I knew Patna would never let me be who I wanted to
be—*needed* to be—in order to thrive. For that, I needed the world.

———— ◦ ————

Chapter 3

〜

I *didn't know how complicated* that world truly was until I became old enough to put all the pieces together. Slowly, as I entered an American grade school and began to understand conversations overheard at the dinner table with a more robust vocabulary, I understood who those strangers were who slept on our floors and shared dinner with my family over the years.

For centuries, India was an extremely large landmass whose borders stretched from Afghanistan to China. A multitude of religions, sects, and cultures cohabitated with relative ease. The British had ruled India for centuries, and my history teachers taught us stories of the revolutionaries who attempted to overthrow the Empire and make our country independent and free.

My favorite was Mahatma Gandhi. I thought his idea of using nonviolence as a way to fight against the British was brilliant. Through assessing the risks of warfare, Gandhi realized India couldn't defeat the British army in battle. Instead, he saw that India *could* defeat the British in the marketplace—because India was Britain's biggest customer. If Indians stopped buying British goods, we would inflict such financial pain on our rulers that Britain, a small island halfway around the world, would have to capitulate. Through nonviolent protests, sit-ins, hunger strikes, and national boycotts of goods, two things happened. British factories began shutting their doors due to lack of demand, and homegrown Indian companies began to take their place. Gandhi taught Indians how to make their own salt from the Indian Ocean and weave their own textiles from locally grown cotton. Indian car companies replaced British ones, and the Indian economy shifted to Indian-run, Indian-owned commerce.

I was deeply affected by the lesson Gandhi taught India and the world when the British Empire succumbed and granted us independence. There was power in business. Household goods, seemingly boring or trivial, held the power to topple governments. Commerce was the lifeblood of society, and I began to look at my father with pride, knowing that his thriving sports business was one more Indian-run business. He too was a hero. He toiled every day to keep his family fed and happy.

But there was a dark undercurrent to these stories too. The strangers in our house weren't just neighbors or friends down on their luck. They were political and religious refugees. As India inched toward independence, two factions in our government began to quarrel over how this new country should look. The Muslim contingent demanded their own country wholly separate from India. In one of their last major decisions as rulers of our land, the British agreed to divide us into two. The piece they partitioned off, now called Pakistan, would be the home of a new Muslim nation. Each country would be its own sovereign country with its own leaders and government.

The Indian Partition of 1947 devastated our country, especially the region of Punjab, the land of Sialkot and my family heritage. The region was split in half along a new national boundary, and soon, Muslims began to migrate west into Pakistan Punjab, while Hindus and Sikhs migrated east into Indian Punjab, Bihar, and other states. Neither government was prepared for such upheaval, and it is estimated that two hundred thousand to two million people were slaughtered during the migrations. Hardly any Hindus or Sikhs remained in the newly created Pakistan, with nearly five million moving east, abandoning their homes and family lands in the process. These refugees flooded Patna and other cities in Northern India. These were the strangers my parents housed, fed, and commiserated with when I was a child.

It angered me that such injustice could exist in the world. I was spoiled, almost, by my parents' strict ethics. It was a major blow to me as a young man to realize not everyone lived up to the same standards. I heard stories about family friends who weren't allotted a home or land after they fled their homes in Sialkot and neighboring cities, even though the government had promised them they would. I saw men discuss shady deals in the markets, and knew from my father's stories with his friends that there was rampant corruption throughout the city of Patna. Now that the British were gone and India had its independence—somehow becoming bloody despite Gandhi's nonviolent teachings—the country was wild and free, and those without scruples preyed on the weak to enrich themselves and their families. The solidarity of "for India, by India" dissipated in the lawless new normal, where the violence and political upheaval made everyone look out only for themselves.

These stories made me resent Patna. It gave me a bad taste in my mouth whenever I overheard my father complaining about a crooked businessman to my mother. I learned early to keep a wary eye on anyone outside of my circle of family members and alleyway friends. I remember when I was a teenager on especially hot days, I'd walk three miles with my friends to the banks of the Ganges to cool off near the moving waters. Biharis lined the shore, walking into the water to cleanse themselves of their sins. *No amount of water will wash away all the corruption in this town*, I thought, *unless the entire city washed downstream in an epic flood.*

I wanted to start fresh—somewhere far away from the bad business of Patna. Sure, I could stay here and become another sly businessman around town and possibly end up with one of those big houses in a rich neighborhood surrounded by walled gardens. But I'd still be sitting behind a wall, waiting for the flood to come.

No, I needed out.

And that out I knew was through the most powerful tool in a person's life: education.

I'd study my way to freedom.

———◆———

Chapter 4

~

Luckily, *I grew up in a family* that prized education and understood its worth. Just as my father helped his siblings gain admission to the schools in Patna, he did the same for his children. My two eldest brothers went to medical school, my third brother became a scientist, and my sisters (rare for the time period) graduated from university with an arts degree and a biology degree. My father also supported my siblings in meeting potential life partners and getting them married off. As the youngest, I saw all of this transpire in front of me like a mirror that revealed my future. I too would get a degree, I too would marry, and I too would settle and have a family of my own.

But my spirit rebelled. I wanted a family, yes, but not in Patna. I knew that if I were to leave this place, I would need all the tools I could get. So, I threw myself into my education. My father enrolled me and my older brother, Harendra, in a local Catholic school called St. Xavier's High School—the best preparatory academy in the city. Because Patna's universities were well known, institutions in England and America set up their own schools to teach the locals as well. Of course, they had ulterior motives of converting us to Christianity, but on the bright side, they brought excellent educators. While other Catholic missionary schools in cities like Calcutta and Darjeeling catered only to Catholic Anglo-American students, St. Xavier's was founded to teach Indian students of all religious backgrounds. Plus, the school was affiliated with Cambridge University in England, which gave it prestige. I'd dream about getting a degree with "Cambridge University" written in it in calligraphy and imagined living in England one day.

The one drawback was the expense. In those days, sometimes we had to take vegetables out on loan from merchants who trusted and knew my parents would pay them back once they had the money. Due to my father's stature in the community, school officials afforded him concessions, such as deferring tuition payments as needed. However, this situation was sustainable for only so long.

One day, my father called my brother and me together to discuss a difficult decision he had made with my mother behind closed doors. The family couldn't afford for both of us to be enrolled at the school anymore. By birthright, Harendra should be chosen to stay enrolled, but my father had other plans.

"Ramesh, you will stay at St. Xavier's. As for you, Harendra, you'll be put in public school." I was seized with guilt. Me? No, Harendra should have been chosen to stay in prep school—tradition, culture, and respect for an older sibling demanded it. I began to protest, but I was stopped by the raised palm of our father's hand.

"My decision is final."

I worried what Harendra might say as we walked out of the room, but after we were dismissed, Harendra turned to me with a smile and whispered, "Excellent!" His enthusiasm caught me by surprise, but he quickly explained that public school was way easier than St. Xavier's. And he was right. Soon, he was sneaking off and skipping classes whenever he liked. My father never pressured him to study hard or disciplined him, and Harendra found himself with more time to focus on his new passion: the family business.

I, meanwhile, loved school and threw myself into my studies. I was at the top of my class and won medals in poetry and drama. I took math, physics, Hindi, English literature, chemistry, and Bible studies. I also played sports, and I found myself pretty good at the three most popular sports in India: cricket, badminton, and soccer. But what really obsessed me was table tennis. I loved to play every evening with a group of guys that included my best friend, Jai Prakash. We'd play for hours. He'd never go anywhere without me. We'd gather at a local community center and play deep into the night. It became an escape from the crowded city, and soon, a way for me to cope with more than just worries about homework or a schoolgirl crush. It became an outlet for dealing with illness and death.

Chapter 5

~

When I was thirteen, my middle brother, Yogendra, was diagnosed with bone cancer in his right leg. Yogendra was smart and athletic. I remember watching him teach younger students in his spare time. With warmth and humor, he'd help poor students study for high school exams so they could get into good colleges, and he never asked for a dime in payment. He excelled in STEM classes and started a business, which he ran on the side. Plus, he was a great badminton player. He competed in national championships, and I'd watch him perform in front of crowds. Their loud cheers would ring in my ears when he made a good shot, and I'd smile with pride. He was my role model and my hero. I'd be blessed if I grew up to be like him.

He was twenty-one years old when he got the diagnosis, and I recall the day he finally had to quit badminton. He was limping then, and the pain showed on his face in a scowl as he walked. Somehow, he kept his spirits up, and by cracking jokes and listening to us talk over dinner, he kept our spirits up too. He didn't let us feel bad for him; instead, he would reassure us he would be fine.

My father took him to specialists around India, and they decided it best to amputate his leg below the knee. I could tell Yogendra was nervous when my parents took him into the hospital, but he patted my head and told me not to worry. I remember him coming back home with a pair of crutches and his leg wrapped in white gauze like a mummy. He was in and out of sedation as he dealt with the pain, and our house, usually so boisterous with laughter and voices, stayed quiet most days.

Yogendra only lasted one more year until the disease spread and took him, bodily, into the earth. We were all in quiet agony. I had lost my hero; my father and mother had lost their shining son. It was a huge shock to us. We had constantly hoped for his improvement. We'd bet our lives on his recovery. We'd never accepted any other option. Until we were forced to accept the truth—Yogendra was gone.

My father took it hard. He smoked more than usual and sat silently in the dark as my mother prepared dinner each night and I did my homework. I'd leave the house to play table tennis with my friends, and when I got home, my father would be in the same place where I'd left him. He hadn't moved an inch. Soon, he too went into the hospital—it was like his heart broke into small pieces and he couldn't figure out how to glue them back together. I remember going to visit him every day after school. In a soft voice, he taught me English lessons: how to write, how to pronounce each word correctly. I hated those lessons at the time; I was eager to get out of the dark and quiet hospital full of illness and wails of sadness and lose myself in table tennis. Unaware at the time, my father was helping me escape Patna through those lessons. In his hospital room, I sharpened the complex and difficult tool of the English language—the language of business around the world.

My father died soon after of a heart attack. I was sixteen. He was cremated according to the Hindu tradition, and we mourned his loss as a family for fourteen days. After, we were left to navigate our lives in Patna without a rudder. Harendra and I took turns caring for our mother as I finished high school and my brother assessed what to do with our father's business. As I took my sadness and channeled it into table tennis, I became a state champion and traveled the country competing in national championships. Harendra supported me, saying "go—win for us!" whenever I hesitated leaving him and my mother at home. We were still children doing the best we could with this new reality without Yogendra and without our father.

One day, after returning from a championship, Harendra told me he'd offered our uncle partnership in the family business. I trusted my brother's judgment and soon busied myself in applying to college and studying for exams. Not long after, I would hear arguments in our house when I got home between my brother and uncle.

"Uncle, you're treating us poorly," Harendra said, "and I know you're not sharing the profits fairly."

"If you're so unhappy, why don't we split the business so you and your brother can run it the way you want, and I'll do the same? It'll save me some grief not having to hear you nag me all the time!" I was furious my uncle spoke to Harendra that way, but we decided to get rid of him and take the small portion he allotted us. My brother and I devised a plan so that I could go to the Bihar College of Engineering and he and I would run the business together. "But you must finish school," he told me. "That's what Dad would have wanted."

I can't describe how impressed I was with Harendra's salesman skills. He could charm anyone on the block, but even then, times were tough. We got by on the meager earnings from the business, but just barely. After a lengthy discussion during my first year of engineering college—which I was awarded a government grant to attend—Harendra and I decided to have our mother and sister move in with one of our older brothers, who worked as a doctor near Delhi. With his larger salary, he could take better care of them and afford to send my sister to college.

After their move-out, Harendra and I found ourselves living a bachelor's life. Our family home felt huge with just two of us living there. Most of our financial strain eased, and I fell into a routine of school, then work, then tennis. Harendra would travel most of the month to keep the sporting goods business afloat, and each day when I'd come home to an empty house, I would sit and daydream about leaving India. I *had* to make it happen. I had fewer and fewer ties to Patna, and I knew I would never be happy there. I would read newspaper articles that told me stories of people's lives in London, Toronto, and New York City. I listened to radio shows from Australia and imagined the gleaming cities there: Melbourne and Sydney. With a firm grasp of the English language, I began to plot my way to a country that spoke it—a country less corrupt, full of freedom and opportunity to find my way to the top, and a place where integrity and honesty were esteemed and not laughed at like in this town. I wanted to get away from the uncles of India—I wanted space to explore the vast world of technology and production. It drew me like the smell of a large feast after a long and difficult fast.

———

Chapter 6

❧

It *was 1968 and the world was changing*, and I was changing too. I had graduated from Bihar College with an engineering degree and was teaching at the University of Patna. Companies began headhunting me with offers for well-paying positions. When I won an award for the Best Teacher in Bihar, I thought I'd use it as leverage to get into an engineering university outside of India, but I soon learned most of those schools only accepted students from wealthy families. As my teaching career soared, I got depressed. The fear grew in me that I'd never make my dream come true, that I'd be stuck teaching in Patna forever.

I talked to Harendra whenever he was back home from business trips. We looked at maps and thought of every option—the U.K. was at the top of my list since I had graduated with a Cambridge University degree. Next were Canada and Australia, which I thought were perfectly fine places to end up in, but from everything I read, only the United States of America was interested in engineers. I didn't have family in these places already, which made it harder, but my friend, Parmatma Saran, was studying psychology at Columbia University in Manhattan, and that contact gleamed in my periphery. *If only I could get to New York*, I'd think, anxiously tossing in my sheets before falling asleep.

One night, while playing a match of table tennis, Jai Prakash told me that he heard that the U.S. Embassy was offering work visas to Indians.

"What's the catch?" I joked, thinking it too good to be true.

"You've heard about the Vietnam War? Well, to get a visa, you have to sign a contract that you'll go to war if you get conscripted."

The plastic ball went sailing past my frozen paddle. I'd heard of the war—there were news articles about protests in the U.S., and the general consensus was that neither side would win anytime soon. *But I'd get a U.S. visa*, I thought. *I could finally leave Patna.* My mind raced to list the pros and cons of making this potentially dangerous deal with the U.S. government.

"Are you considering it?" Jai laughed. "It's suicide!"

When I got home that night, Harendra was gone, and I remember not sleeping a wink. *This is it—this is my chance. What am I willing to risk getting that chance?*

The next day, I walked over to the U.S. Embassy and waited my turn until an officer asked what I wanted.

"I want to apply to work in the United States."

The officer looked me up and down. "Are you sure?"

"Yes, I'm sure."

"I don't know if you are. Most Indians walk away after I tell them what they have to do to get a visa. You will be required to enroll in the Selective Service the moment you land in the U.S. Are you willing to put your life on the line for the U.S. of A.?"

"Sure," I said. It might have sounded flippant to the officer, whose eyes widened at my answer, but I was young and brash. "I'm here to apply for a visa," I continued. "If you accept me, great, I'll buy a one-way ticket as soon as possible. I don't care what it takes—I want to live there. The United States will become my new home, my new country, and my new fatherland. And I will fight to protect my fatherland."

The officer walked over to his superior at the back of the room. The superior officer glanced at me as I patiently sat in the chair against the wall. I was surprised at how calm I felt—it was as if the walls of the embassy disappeared and I could see my new life in New York City, the bustling and orderly streets filled with well-dressed businessmen going to work in tall towers, all striving toward greatness, and I too would soon join them.

"What's wrong with him?" I heard the superior officer say, his voice rising over the hushed conversation underway.

"I don't know," the officer replied, "but he's willing to join the army for his visa."

"Well, what are you waiting for? Sign up the bastard!"

The officer walked back over to his desk and pulled out a thin stack of forms. I signed my name without even reading the fine print, and the officer stamped the visa right in front of my eyes.

I was free.

———◦———

Chapter 7

$F_{our\ months\ later\ in\ December\ 1968}$, I found myself on a one-way flight to the United States. Harendra had bought me the cheapest ticket he could find—on credit. After I received the visa, I still didn't know how I'd afford to travel, but Harendra, in his ever-patient and scheming wisdom, said, "Don't worry, I'll find a way. There's always a way." For weeks, Harendra drove through Patna on his scooter visiting every friend, near-relative, business acquaintance, and passerby and said: "Let's get Ramesh to America! Yes, yes, of course I'll pay you back." I was energized by the community's support for me, and my brother's belief in my dream too. I knew if it wasn't for his enthusiasm and innate salesmanship, I would have never left India. He borrowed every cent I needed, then conspired with a travel agent friend to book me a ticket.

"Harendra, how will I pay everyone back?" I said once the ticket was in my hand, very real and very much out of my budget. I was soon to be a "NINJA": no income, no job, no assets. I was twenty-three years old.

I was moving to a country I'd never set foot in before. More than my own well-being, I was caught in worry for everyone who had chipped in to get me there.

"Don't worry, brother," he reassured me. "I'll figure it out."

We set out to exchange our Indian rupees for U.S. dollars and bought cheap clothes—light slacks, thin button-down shirts, and a few ties. My excitement was infectious. Harendra and I drank each night and played table tennis with friends and spent my last week in celebration for my unknown, thrilling future.

We kept my plans a secret from our siblings and mother. I was nervous enough—I couldn't afford to carry their fears and worries as well. My neighbors were shocked at the risk I was taking.

"You have a great job here, Ramesh," they said.

"You have a bright future in Patna."

"What will you do if you can't find work?"

"I'll find work, no matter what," I told them, "even if it means being a janitor!"

"Planes are very dangerous," my neighbor said with concern in his eyes.

"It may fall from the sky," his wife continued.

"Keep your belongings close and hide your money," Jai Prakash warned. "People are going to pickpocket you. You can't trust anyone."

The nervous babble of conversation swirled in my head as I drove to the airport. An officer at the airline gate ordered me to carry all my immigration documents in my hand. "Do not pack them in your luggage," he said.

I looked at the Kuwait Airways ticket in my hand. On the bottom, in a light blue stripe, were images of famous buildings around the world. Above it in blazing red swooped a large jumbo jet. I smiled, knowing I was about to be in that jet jumping from city to city around the world. My itinerary took me from Patna to Delhi to Bombay to Kuwait to London to Paris, where I decided to spend a couple nights on holiday (it was included in the price of the ticket, so why not?)—then to my final destination in New York City. The number of cities and transfers made my head spin, and so I put my visa in my checked bag for safekeeping. When I got to Paris, I could hand-carry it into the U.S.

On the plane, my thoughts began to whirl around me like a dust storm that blocked out the sun. I breathed and let the dust settle. "I'm headed to a bright future," I told myself. "My destiny is in my hands now, and no one else's. Nobody else is to blame for what becomes of me. I am finally free." But another thought nagged at me. I was in the middle of taking the biggest risk of my life. I was giving up everything— my family, friends, a stable job and career in Patna—to follow my dreams; I might be conscripted into a war I knew little about and die. I had a handful of cash and no other financial support. I had nowhere to live when I landed. And yet, the risk felt worthwhile, because I knew, if it all fell to pieces, I could get a job, any job. I would find a way to live, to work, even if it meant I started from nothing. I'd clean toilets just so I could get a foothold in the United States. It was a risk that I calculated over and over in my head. And I knew I could incur a bit of loss, but the gains would be infinite.

As the plane flew over India, I looked down at the brown fields and brown villages and brown cities of my country—my old country. I didn't feel a pang of remorse or tinge of sadness. I was happy to leave it all behind. As my plane

CALCULATED RISK #1:

Moving to a new country with nothing other than tenacity and a dream.

hopped from Patna to Delhi to Bombay to Kuwait, I had no idea I would be visiting these cities twenty-five years later, flying first class as the president of the largest flexible duct business in the world. I was just a young man with ambitions that were big enough to crowd out the fear of leaving everything I knew for something unexpected—something I'd risk everything to get.

Chapter 8

I *landed in London toward the end of December,* tired and sore from countless hours sitting upright in the plane. I stood at baggage claim as all the other people on my flight retrieved their bags until there was only a handful of passengers left watching the metal belt turn in circles. A scattering of unclaimed bags revolved in front of me. I began to panic. I walked to the airline help desk, and the representative reassured me everything would be okay. "Just wait a little longer," she said, and so I walked back over to the belt and stood until the last bag arrived. It wasn't mine.

"Miss," I said to the representative, "my bag didn't arrive!"

"These things happen. Please be patient. We'll do everything we can to locate your bag."

"But you don't understand!" I yelled. "All my travel documents are in my bag."

"Please, sir, be patient. We will do our best to locate your bag."

I could tell at that point that her kindness was turning to strained tolerance. I paced back and forth in front of her desk. My visa was in that bag! *I'll never get it back*, I thought. *I can't get into the U.S. without it.* The officer had warned me the visa was good for four months. If I arrived a day after that allotted time, I would be denied entry. I quickly calculated the last day I could enter the U.S. was . . . in two days! If I didn't get my papers and into New York City in forty-eight hours, my trip would be canceled, and I'd have to find a way to get back to Patna. All these years of waiting, all my hard work would go to waste. My dreams would be shattered.

"Mr. Bhatia," the airline representative interrupted my spiraling thoughts. "I've sent a Telex message to Kuwait. They've located your bag." I smiled so large it hurt my face. "It will arrive on the next flight, which arrives tomorrow morning." I was relieved but still, my anxiety hounded me. *What if the suitcase doesn't arrive? What if the baggage handler makes a mistake? What if? What if?*

"Do you need a place to stay for the night?" the woman asked. "I can help reserve a hotel for you."

"Yes, please," I replied.

Lost in thought, I walked through Heathrow Airport and outside to the waiting taxis. As a blast of cold air rushed through the opening doors, I realized another problem: all my clothes were in that bag too. And, being a boy from the intense heat of Patna, I had no idea how cold a December day in London could be. I was freezing. I had, at most, one hundred dollars to get me settled in the U.S. I hated to part with any of it frivolously, but the clothes I had on weren't enough to keep me warm. So, after checking into my hotel, I took a bus to find a coat. After leaving a few shops I couldn't afford, I found a small storefront with a thin coat on sale. Handing over the twenty-five pounds to the shopkeeper, I felt like I was in a daze. So much money! For this limp thing! That amount of money was a fortune to me, but stepping back into the street, it was worth it. Warmer and able to cut out the stiff winter breeze, my mind was able to return to my even bigger worry: my lost bag floating somewhere between England and the Middle East. I wandered the blocks around my hotel not eating, not drinking, just thinking about that bag and willing it to arrive.

This is all your fault, I told myself. *You're to blame. Your carelessness got you into this mess.* My thoughts circled like sharks smelling blood. "Always keep your documents in your hand," I heard the officer say, over and over. Honestly, though, how was I to know? Rationally speaking, carrying them in my hand was the same as packing them away since I never, in a thousand years, could have imagined my bag could be lost or left behind. I truly believed they were safer in there. *Give it up, Ramesh*, I replied to myself. *This is all your fault. You can't blame anyone but you and your stupidity.*

I didn't sleep a wink that night and got out of bed the minute the sky turned pale. I took a taxi to the airport and sat at baggage claim for three hours awaiting the plane's arrival. *Please be on the plane*, I prayed. *Please be in this group of bags coming out on the carousel.* One by one, bags appeared, and when I saw the worn leather of my bag, I grabbed it to my chest like a long-lost friend. I put it on the floor, took out my papers, and walked over to the Air India counter.

"I want to cancel my flight to Paris," I told them. "Give me a nonstop to New York, the next flight that has a seat." Back then, lots of planes were half-empty with plenty of seats, and they easily booked me on the next flight out early the next morning. I went back to the hotel and enjoyed the first meal since I'd landed in England—a huge one with potatoes and pot pie and a few glasses of red wine. I fell into bed exhausted and immediately began to snore, my visa clutched tightly to my chest.

———•———

Chapter 9

~

To *my surprise, I took my seat* on the Air India plane next to two amiable and jolly Punjabi men, who immediately insisted I join them for a round of scotch—even though it was nine in the morning. Before I knew it, the plane touched down at the John F. Kennedy International Airport, and I went through U.S. customs and immigration with a bit of a buzz. I proudly offered my visa and papers and sighed with relief when they stamped it and hurried me along down the queue. The journey had been tougher on my bag than me, it seemed. Its handle was completely broken, and so I dragged the bag to the sidewalk outside and waited for Parmatma to pick me up. I was happy to have that coat from London, as thin as it was. New York was even colder than London. I stood and watched the cars go by for an hour before I began to get nervous again.

"Excuse me," I said to a tall, gray-haired man in a long wool coat smoking a cigarette. "My friend is supposed to pick me up—he's studying for his PhD at Columbia University—but he's an hour late. I don't know what to do."

"You should call your friend," he said. "There's a payphone right over there." He pointed toward the doors.

"I don't have any coins," I said, my voice cracking with anxiety.

"Here, I'll call for you. What's the number?"

He tried a few times, but no one answered the phone at the other end of the line.

"What should I do?" I asked.

"Do you have his address? Take a taxi to his place."

I didn't have much money left and didn't want to spend it all on one car ride. But I didn't have any other choice. As scared as I was, I told myself, "This is your new country now. Act like an American. Call a cab."

The ride from Brooklyn to Manhattan was mesmerizing. As we approached the island city, the skyline appeared. I'd never seen buildings this tall before. We drove over a bridge, and I looked at the river—it was much tidier than the Ganges but just as brown. As we entered Manhattan, tall gray buildings flew by me in orderly rows. Sometimes, at big intersections, I could see for miles in one direction, the buildings creating a man-made canyon. It was new and even bigger than I'd ever imagined.

The thrill of my new city came crashing down when the cab driver told me the cost of the ride: twenty-five dollars. I was floored. That was 187.50 rupees, or more than a month's rent for two people in a nice apartment in Patna! It was painful to give him that much money. I parted with the money and thanked the driver. He gave me a scowl and drove off. *What was that about?* I thought. *I'd given him a fortune!* I didn't understand how the cab business worked, and in my naiveté I had failed to give him a tip.

In any case, I was anxious to find Parmatma and get out of the bitter cold. The lobby to my friend's building was warm compared to the outside world. A receptionist sat at a desk at the end of the lobby.

"Hello," I said. "I'm here to see Parmatma Saran."

"I'm sorry," she said, "he's gone for the weekend. You'll have to come back later."

I began to panic but didn't want to show the receptionist my fear, so I gathered my broken bag and thin coat and sat down in a chair in the corner where I thought she couldn't see me. For three hours, I stared at the wall and didn't know what to do. I hadn't eaten anything all day, and a breeze chilled me each time a student opened the double doors to the street. But I had no other choice; there were millions of people in this city, and each one of them was a stranger except for Parmatma. Thoughts chased thoughts around my head like yappy dogs, and I kept trying to get them to hush.

Around midnight, the phone rang, and the receptionist answered it. I heard her say, "There is a man waiting here for you. He's been sitting in the corner for hours. Yes, I'll put him on." I jumped up and rushed to take the phone.

"You asshole! Where are you? I've been sitting in this lobby freezing my ass off waiting for you."

"Hey, hey, Ramesh, calm down. You told me in your letter you were flying in from Paris! I went to JFK looking for you, but you weren't there."

"Damn," I whispered. I'd forgotten to tell him that I'd flown straight from London. "I flew in early. What a mix-up. It's totally my fault. But look, Parmatma, it's freezing. Come get me. I have to tell you about my crazy trip. My bag got stuck in Kuwait with my visa in it and—"

"Alright, alright, save it for when I get there. You can tell me over dinner. I'm sure you're starving."

I fell back into the chair, relieved at the thought of a friendly face, a big meal, and a secure place to sleep. As the sun went down in the city and the lights of the lobby flickered on, I felt grateful that the university allowed me one night to stay with my friend. When he arrived, I gave him a giant hug, and we stayed up late into the night, him sitting on his bed, me sitting on a cot, exhausted but excited over reminiscing about India, mutual friends, and Parmatma's extensive knowledge of my new home. I fell asleep after a long journey and dreamed about my future, which was now so close I could touch it.

———•———

Chapter 10

~

The next day, Saran arranged for me to move into a cheap room at 600 West 125th Street in Harlem. It cost thirteen dollars a week, which I thought would get me a pretty swanky spot. Instead, I walked into the smallest, dirtiest room I'd ever seen. Cockroaches scattered across the floor when I opened the door, and one of the windows was left open, making the room feel like an icebox. I tried to close it, but it was broken open, and a cold wind blew across my face. There was no heater or private bathroom; instead, I would have to share a bathroom at the end of the hall with four other tenants. It was a wonder I didn't cry myself to sleep.

"Sat srii akaal," I heard from the hall through my open doorway. A Punjabi man in his early thirties stood across the way, Hindi music playing from within his apartment. "What's your name?"

"I'm Ramesh," I said,

"Are you from the north?" he asked.

"Yes, Patna."

"Patna!" The man yelled and clapped his hands. "We're from Patna! Come in, come in. Who's your father?" He took me by the shoulder and ushered me into his room, where a few other Indian men sat drinking tea. They all smiled and asked questions and demanded I tell them about my journey across the world. Through the gossip and laughter, I felt at home after my long journey. The men promised to cook with me in the communal kitchen and help me find my way around my new city. The sounds of Hindi music calmed me, and even though my room was depressing as hell, I had good company, and I knew I wouldn't feel so alone.

The next morning, I began what became my daily routine: I'd bundle up, still freezing from the cold air blowing through my broken window, leave my apartment at 9 a.m., buy a copy of *The New York Times*, and search the want ads for a job. Then, I'd wander the city equipped with the address of a different company headquarters each day to cold call. I remember walking mile after mile, scouting out the corporate offices of General Motors and Proctor & Gamble. What I soon realized was these companies were *based* in Manhattan, but their actual operations were scattered across the country. I'd walk into the offices and ask for openings, but they turned me away. Every call I made to those small ads in the corner of the newspaper ended with a "sorry" and a dial tone. As the days drew on, I got disheartened. Saran would visit and cheer me up with a long walk to the only Indian restaurant in New York City. At least we could banter and talk about girls until I'd forget about my constant worry.

Three weeks into my new life, I began to run out of money. I found a local diner that served brunch from 11 a.m. to noon for a dollar, and I'd eat there every day. Newspaper, ads, phone calls, walks through Midtown, nothing. Then, I'd do it again, and again—until the day I read a small, two-line ad for a company in Roselle Park. "Seeking recent engineering grad, no exp. necessary. Pay not good." I had no idea where the hell

Roselle Park was, but I quickly gave them a call. The owner listened to me with excitement in his voice.

"I don't care where you came from," he said. "You sound smart and capable, and I'm desperate for help. You should come visit the office for an interview—but first, I have to ask: Will you move to Jersey if I hire you? I can't have you trekking across the Hudson every day, or you'll never be here on time."

"Yes, of course, sir, I'll be happy to move to Jersey," I said, not caring that I didn't know what that meant. He gave me an address and a time and hung up elated.

"New Jersey!" Saran yelled. "I mean, I know you're desperate, but Jersey?"

"What?" I said back. "Who cares? It's a job. It's just over the river. I saw it on a subway map."

"Hoboken is 'just over the river,'" Saran said. "Roselle Park might as well be Bihar State with how long it's going to take you to get there. We'll probably never see each other again. Look, I'll show you. You have to take two trains and then a bus . . ."

I pushed Saran's worry aside and focused on the route Saran explained to me on a paper napkin. When the date and time arrived, I took the train and walked into a one-person office. The man in charge was named Mr. Gardner, and his company was called Marvin B. Gardner Co. He worked in the oil and gas industry as a consultant, and he told me about a project he needed assistance with. It involved a contract with Getty Oil Company, and he wanted me to work full-time as a mechanical engineer to draw up sketches to present to Getty's management team. I had no experience in gas and oil, but I assured him I was a fast learner and a hard worker. "I'll make you proud," I told him, nervous about my inexperience. But desperation favors the unqualified, and he hired me on the spot.

"I can't offer much, though. Your salary would be $175 a week." I quickly calculated that to be around $4.50 an hour. Back in India, that amount would be huge! But here in New York, I had no idea if it was decent or downright dismal.

"I'll think about it," I told him. Since this was the first offer I'd received in the United States, I wanted to make sure I wasn't making a mistake. After shaking hands and leaving the office, I immediately found a payphone and called Saran.

"Mr. Gardner has offered 175 a week. You've been living in New York for a few years. What do you think? Is it acceptable?"

"Hell yes, Ramesh. Take it. Beggars can't be choosers."

On the long ride back home, I thought about my options. In reality, there was only one, which didn't make it much of an option. Rather, it was a requirement. I needed money. I knew I would learn from Mr. Gardner. And who knew where it would lead me?

Back home, I jumped on the communal phone in the lobby of my apartment building and dialed his number.

"Mr. Gardner," I said, "I accept."

"Wonderful!" he said. "Now, let's get you out of Harlem. My wife knows of a place . . ." As he continued to talk, I fell into a deep state of peace. Deeper than any I'd felt since leaving India. Deeper than I'd felt even before then. I couldn't remember the last time I felt this happy, this content. I felt like Hira Lal had given me a chocolate, and I'd just placed it in my mouth. What a blessing, I thought, to be taken care of so well. And by a man I hardly knew! With the phone pressed against my ear, I smiled like a self-satisfied child.

Chapter 11

～

The Sunday before my first day of work, I couldn't sleep. *How am I going to do this job with zero knowledge of gas and energy? Will he see through me and call me incompetent? Will he fire me on the spot? Where are they going to move me? Is there going to be an Indian restaurant nearby? Who will I cook with? Who will spend time with me?*

I maybe got an hour of shut-eye before my alarm rang at 4:30 in the morning. With Saran's napkin in my frozen hand, I put on my clothes. Through my sleepy eyes, now finally opening, I realized the predicament I was in. The city was feet deep in snow. A severe storm had hit the city overnight, and snow continued to fall in silent heaps on the street. My heart sank. *What a nightmare*, I thought, and rushed out of my apartment as soon as I could slip into my thin British-bought coat. As I walked to the station a block down the street, I saw buses stuck in snow; offices and diners were dark. It was like I was the only person alive in New York City that morning. But nothing was going to stop me from my first day of work. I could freeze to death on the way there, but that would be easier for me to handle than being late—or, even worse, not showing up at all.

A train finally arrived and took me to Grand Central, where I transferred to a train headed to Roselle Park Station. There, I walked the mile to the office. The snow had stopped falling, and sharp sunlight fell through the trees, hardening the snow on the ground into sheets of glass. It took me an hour to slip and slide over that icy mile to Mr. Gardner's office, and I was exhausted by the time I reached the door.

I smiled, then turned the handle. It was locked. The windows above me were dark. I had made it right on time—it was 8:26—but Mr. Gardner was nowhere in sight. I huddled in my coat, catching whatever warmth I could feel from the sun on my face, and waited. My new boss showed up at 9:30.

"I'm so sorry for being late, Ramesh! But hell, what are you doing here? You shouldn't have come at all! This weather is something dreadful."

"It's my first day, Mr. Gardner," I said. "I would never miss my first day of work."

Mr. Gardner ushered me into the office, made a hot pot of coffee, and sat me in the corner at a desk. Next to me was a drafting table. I don't know if it was the stark contrast to the cold outside or my lousy apartment uptown, but this warm little corner felt like heaven on earth. I'd never seen anything so beautiful and well appointed. It was clean; sharp pencils and ink pens stood waiting for my imagination in short cups on the desk. Drawers were filled with fresh, blank paper.

"Settle in, Ramesh," Mr. Gardner said. "This is your home away from home now." And he gave me some simple drawings to start with that morning. I took up the pencil and tentatively began my task. My boss was courteous and helpful; whenever I had a question, he would answer without annoyance. All of a sudden it was dark out again, and I'd made quite a dint in his demands.

"I'm starving," Mr. Gardner said. "What are you doing for dinner?"

"I'm not sure, sir," I said hesitantly. "I'll probably grab something back in Harlem."

"But that won't be for another two hours with the commute ahead of you! Come with me to my place tonight. I'll phone my wife to add a seat for you."

"Oh, thank you, sir," I said, excited about my first home-cooked meal in America. Mr. Gardner lived nearby, and his two sons and wife joined us that night. They had lots of questions about India and my culture, and I told them stories about Patna, my family, table tennis, and my long journey to their country. The boys sat rapt as I described Hindu history. "Imagine," I said, "my ancestry goes back two thousand years in India, and many of my beliefs and habits originated with them and were passed down through countless generations."

"It makes America feel like a young buck," one of the sons said.

"Your country is young," I agreed. "Young and full of life, just like a teenager. I'm happy to be in a place that feels so fresh."

After a few glasses of wine, I was beaming. Even though our cultures were so different, I felt at ease in their warm attention and cozy home.

———•———

Chapter 12

~

S*oon, I moved to a new apartment* in Roselle Park that Mr. Gardner's wife had found for me, which cut my commute by 90 percent. It was easy to get to the office and work long hours, and after a few days, I learned Mr. Gardner's business like the back of my hand. My new boss treated me as an equal, asking me my opinion on how to best tackle our project for Getty. Our shared penchant for working late into the night brought us very close, and we began brainstorming about a new project and even some inventions Mr. Gardner was eager to develop. I channeled my background knowledge in engineering and found myself quite engaged with my boss's ideas, sometimes arguing against a dumb idea or misstep in his thinking. We'd spar, but it was always respectful, no matter how heated our conversations became. It felt like a game of table tennis, just with ideas instead of paddles.

"I appreciate your candidness, Ramesh," he told me one evening. "It's rare to find an employee who isn't afraid to speak his mind. And you've got quite a sharp one."

I blushed with pride. I wished my father was around so I could tell him how much my new boss appreciated me. But as it was, not only did I not have my father around, I had no one. Each evening, I walked home to an empty apartment. I didn't even have a TV to distract me. I remember those being hard nights. I'd sit at home and cry. I missed my friends, my brother, my tennis pals. The new apartment was much nicer than the one in Harlem, but at least at my old place I had a community and my Patna floor mates, and Saran was nearby. Here, in this faraway Jersey town, I'd think of my family on the other side of the world and write them letters. Sometimes, they would grow to five or six pages long as I described my job, my boss, the weather, the buildings in Roselle Park, the food (a bit bland), and the wine (very good!). It was a lonely time for me. Evenings stretched long, as if every minute took five to pass by. Even so, I never regretted my decision to come here. It cheered me a bit to think I was so far away from the *hera pheri*, or funny business, so common in Patna. Mr. Gardner was a respectable businessman, and everyone I met worked within an unspoken system of utmost decorum. People here knew the rules of the game, and I was eager to learn them too.

Over the next few months, Mr. Gardner took me to inspect chemical plants in Bayonne and Jersey City. He pointed out the mechanics of chemical processing, the machines and tools used in each step, and how the plants dealt with waste and worker safety. Our work for Getty went so well, Mr. Gardner hired another engineer to assist us. The man was a bit older than me and kind enough. His assistance took some burden off my daily schedule, but he didn't much care for me. He especially bristled at my tendency to work late. "We should get paid overtime for any work we do after 6 p.m.," he told me when Mr. Gardner stepped out for lunch. "It's unfair."

"I disagree," I told him. "The more time you spend in the office, the more you get to learn from an expert in our field. I bet you'd learn more from Mr. Gardner spending an extra hour on the clock than any school in Manhattan."

My coworker disagreeably mumbled, his face screwed up in distaste, and got back to work.

He didn't last all of three months.

Now, I wasn't a brownnoser, and I wasn't lying to that engineer either. I knew the more facetime I got with my boss, the better my skills would grow. I was thirsty for knowledge, and the work was fascinating. I mean, in that little office over a bank in a small suburban Jersey town, we worked on projects that had never been conceived before. We worked at the forefront of what was possible with oil and gas, and with our weekly spars, constantly plotted and planned new avenues for the future of energy and how the world might become better, more efficient, and more profitable.

One such project was to figure out a way to transport oil from Prudhoe's Bay in Alaska to the lower fifty states in the U.S. without causing environmental damage. We spitballed ideas and drew hasty drawings, exciting each other over the possibilities. As my boss and I talked, I drew a complex underground transport and storage system that connected the frozen Arctic seas to the warm Seattle harbor. We discussed temperature constraints and how altitude affects the way gas flows through pipelines.

Sadly, we weren't given an opportunity to put these ideas into practice. Our plan would have required the support of a huge company with hefty capital. But as we worked, I learned and absorbed, sopping up every lesson my boss shared with me like a sponge.

———•———

Chapter 13

❧

A *year went by, and Mr. Gardner and I celebrated* the end of our project together. It was around Christmastime toward the end of 1970, and the streetlamps were festooned with fake green wreaths. We just wrapped up some final paperwork, and my boss pulled out a nice bottle of whiskey and two rocks glasses.

"Ramesh," he said, "let's have a drink to celebrate." He handed me a glass and held his up high. "I love the work we've done together. I couldn't have done it without you." But there was a sadness in his eyes as he spoke.

"Thank you, sir. But what's wrong?"

"I don't have any more work for you to do with me. I tried to find other projects, but they haven't materialized."

I sat down in my office chair, whiskey in my hand, and didn't take a sip. "So . . ." I started.

"Ramesh, I'm sorry. I have to let you go."

I was devastated. Am I really going to start over again? Find a new job? I'd saved some money from working with Mr. Gardner, but I didn't have much. Anxiety crept up my spine and I took the glass of whiskey and downed it in one swallow.

"You're a smart young man," he said to me, his glass still full. "You'll figure something out. In the meantime, since I'm not firing you but laying you off from a lack of work, you can apply for unemployment benefits." As he talked, he pulled out an info sheet and handed it to me. I folded it up and put it in my pocket, thanked him, but I couldn't quite hear his words. I was stuck somewhere deep inside me that was filled with disappointment.

I walked home that evening with a mind full of sharks. *That last job was a fluke*, my mind told me. *You were just lucky. You won't find another one this time. How are you going to pay rent? Your apartment in Roselle Park is much more expensive than the one in Harlem. You're going to have to move back to that dingy room without heat and beg for work.* I got home and lay on my bed without eating any dinner. I stared at the ceiling and lost myself in my racing thoughts, until at some point, sleep took me from my worry, and I forgot my sadness in dreams.

The next morning, over a cup of coffee, I unfolded the piece of paper Mr. Gardner had given me. It had information for a local Social Security Office where I could go and apply for unemployment. *What is this?* I thought. *This can't be for me.*

I phoned Saran and told him about my predicament. "Go get that money," he said. "It's a brilliant thing about this country. It was created for people exactly like you."

I didn't believe him, but I went to appease Saran. I filled out some forms, and a few days later, a check came in the mail. For doing nothing! I felt a wave of guilt run through me. *I don't deserve this. A man should work for his paycheck.* It felt dirty, somehow, like I was stealing from someone. But Saran assured me that the U.S. government created this program to help people in transition between jobs. "So you can eat and pay rent and keep healthy to find your next job. Think about it; if you didn't have money, you'd stop buying coffee at your bodega and groceries at the market. It's not just an infusion of cash for you. It's for your local businesses too."

That made sense to me. What a brilliant idea! Plus, the government got some of that money back through sales tax, and I did pay a decent amount of my wages to income tax to the IRS. I realized this weekly check wasn't a kind of theft; rather, it was a community protection program, something that every citizen could utilize in a time of need. *India has nothing like this*, I thought. Back home, if I lost my job and couldn't pay rent, I'd be on the street.

Still, I wanted to work, and the $300 a month only stretched so far. So, I focused my sights on finding another job in the oil and gas industry, since I could leverage the skills and experience I'd gained with Mr. Gardner in the field. Instead of scouring the newspapers like I had a year ago, I contacted a few employment agencies in the city who were kept on retainer by employers looking for skilled workers.

Soon, I landed an interview with a company called Frederic R. Harris, Inc. They were looking to hire a trainee engineer with experience in oil and gas. The conversation went well enough; the men in the room seemed to like me and what I had to say. They were even impressed with my ideas for how to move the industry forward with future projects. Afterward, as the other men left the room, the manager walked up to me.

"Ramesh," he said, "I'm going to be frank. My superiors instructed me not to hire any foreigners. You're notorious for not being loyal, you see? But there's something about you that's . . . different." I held my breath. "I'm willing to take a chance on you. When can you start?"

Flustered, I said, "Tomorrow, sir." He smiled and shook my hand.

"Good," he said. "Now, prove me right, you hear? Or it's not just your ass on the line. It's mine too."

"You won't regret this, sir," I said, shaking his hand. "I promise you that."

———◦———

Chapter 14

Winter *was ending when I landed a job* at Frederick R. Harris, and, as luck would have it, New York City had the biggest snowstorm of 1971 the night before my first day of work—again. Trains and busses across the boroughs were running late or canceled. Feeling like my life was stuck on repeat, I got out of bed, stared into the snow, and breathed to give me the strength to get myself to the office that morning on time—no matter what. I wasn't going to let some xenophobic coworkers have any excuse to talk down to me or whisper about my laziness. I was going to show up early every day, do my job, say "yes" and "please" and "thank you," all because I knew, deep down, that I was still at the very beginning of my career, and I had a long way to go to get to the top. *It's all part of the game*, I thought, and I knew I was going to win.

Funnily enough, I now lived in New Jersey and had to commute to Midtown Manhattan. My new office building was at E. 42nd Street and Second Avenue, and my commute again became monstrous. I walked a mile from my apartment to Journal Square, took a bus to the Port

Authority, and transferred to a crosstown train. I left my apartment at 6 a.m. and got to the office building at 8:30.

The office was practically empty that morning, and my manager told me I shouldn't have come in, but I said: "What is a little snow?" and he smiled and showed me to my new desk. The company was a huge step up from Mr. Gardner's two-person operation in Roselle Park. FRH employed around one hundred engineers. Each day I met new coworkers, and they ranged from locals to immigrants from Italy, Colombia, Poland, Yugoslavia, Greece, and other countries. I had a nagging thought at the back of my head. *Why did my manager say they didn't trust foreigners when there are a handful of them on staff? Was it because I am foreign, or because I am Indian?* I quickly noticed I was the only Indian at the office, but I brushed the thought aside. *If they don't trust me*, I thought, *I can't wait to prove them wrong.*

Frederic R. Harris Inc. was a world leader in the design of oil and petrochemical plants around the world. Most oil companies would consult with FRH to design new and unique installations in various countries. Before I was hired, the company designed the biggest and best offshore terminals for oil extraction and storage in Saudi Arabia, Iran, Singapore, Canada, and other countries.

As I began my work as a trainee, I'd hear senior executives talk about their upcoming trips to countries around the world. They'd meet clients and discuss details about their contracts, deals, and constructions. *What a glamorous life*, I thought as I drew my diagrams and assisted on projects that began to pile up on my desk. Just like with Mr. Gardner, I arrived early, stayed late, and learned everything I could about FRH's projects and the complex business of managing a global company. There were many moving parts, with workers doing multiple and simultaneous tasks to complete projects for different clients. The office ran smoothly, and everyone seemed to be relatively happy with their role in this giant organism. I put my skills to work: engineering skills from college, English from elementary school and my father, punctuality and respectfulness from my grandfather, and humor from my mother. I'd joke with my coworkers and chat with them over coffee. I got to know as many people in the office as I could. I'd see some workers who kept to themselves, and I didn't want to be like them. That would make management suspicious. And besides, I was a pretty social guy and loved to chat. I knew from watching Harendra work his clients back in Patna how far a congenial, charming personality could take you. I smiled, I laughed, I inquired. And slowly, slowly, I won over the other workers in the office.

A turning point came when a coworker invited me to join the company bowling league. I began playing with the team every Friday evening, and we'd go out after for dinner and drinks. We'd swap jokes and poke fun at each other's home countries, and then talk about our shared goals for a better future. It felt, sometimes, like a mini-United Nations at the office. We became very close.

"You know," I told a colleague one night, "bowling is fun, but you should see me at table tennis." I gestured to a table near the bar.

"You mean ping-pong?" He laughed. "C'mon, Ramesh, ping-pong is a kid's game."

"You think so, do you?" I replied. "I bet I'll beat you before you get a single point."

"You're on," he said, and we got some balls and paddles and took our positions. Within three minutes, I beat him 11–0.

"Dammit," my coworker yelled, slamming his paddle on the table.

"Don't be a sore loser," I teased, "it's just a kid's game, right?"

"Rematch," he said, picking up the paddle. "Let's go."

His exasperated grunts caught the attention of our colleagues and drew them away from the bowling lane to our table. They watched, mouths open, as I again beat my coworker 11–0.

"Jesus, Holy Mary, and Joseph," another coworker whispered, "you're good as hell, Ramesh."

"I was a champion back home," I said, smiling. "But I haven't played since moving here from India."

"I wanna play you," another man said.

"No, give me a turn—I can beat you," said another. By the end of the night, I had beaten them all. A wave of respect moved through them. "Ramesh, the master of table tennis," they said. And soon, a bit tipsy on beer, we schemed a way to make our workdays a bit more fun.

We convinced our manager to install a table tennis table in the break room at work, and every lunchtime, we'd convene for friendlies. Our laughter would permeate the office, and during that first round of games the office manager stopped by in the doorway.

"Ramesh," he said to me when we all filed back to our desks, "you're good. Like, damn good. I've got an idea that could make us a bit of cash . . ." We talked in a hush and shook hands on a new deal that had nothing to do with oil or gas. The deal went like this: My manager would hustle people in the office to play me at lunch. Buy-in was low, around three to five dollars a game, but if they lost, they'd have to pay, and the manager and I would split the winnings 50/50. We soon had a nice betting ring going on every day, and I relished the thrill of winning and the reputation, which spread quickly through the ranks, of being a sports champion. The money was fun, but that recognition meant even more for me. I gained respect from coworkers and managers whom I had failed to win over with my banter and niceties. Executives who didn't know me from my Colombian coworker learned my name. Not only that, but I earned special privileges around the office. My manager (ahem, betting agent) became a loyal confidant and always had my back.

Of course, I know my engineering skills and sharp mind brought me success at FRH, but I suspect my table tennis playing helped open some doors too. I thought back to when I was a teenager and how some of my aunts and uncles shook their heads at my obsessive playing, saying it was just a distraction. But here, at a global powerhouse company in Manhattan, I was winning over people's respect and confidence. Soon, I had a seat at the table and was included in critical decision-making. Within a year, I got a promotion to lead engineer with six employees under my supervision—some of whom had been at FRH longer than me.

All my skills led me here, and I was a hit.

———•———

Chapter 15

One day, my boss called me into the office. I sat down, and he looked at me with a concerned look on his face.

"How do you feel about travel?" he asked.

"I don't mind it so much, as long as someone else deals with the visa part."

"We have a project in Singapore, and . . ." He kept speaking, but I couldn't focus on his words. Singapore! ". . . Ramesh?" I came to, my boss staring at me.

"Oh, yessir. Yessir. I would love to go."

"I'm choosing Greg Jones to assist you."

"But, sir," I started.

"Is something the matter?"

"Greg has seniority here. Are you sure you don't want me to assist him?"

"Ramesh," he said, one hand on my shoulder, "this is business in America, not India. Seniority be damned. It's a simple equation. You're smarter and better at your job than Greg. He works for *you* now."

I went back into the office beaming with pride but worried about Greg's reaction to the news. As I expected, a few friends mentioned Greg grumbling over lunch about being assigned to assist a "newbie." But as the trip approached, Greg walked up to my desk and shook my hand. "Management has been singing your praises," he said. "I was sore to think I'd have to work for you, but if what they say is true, I'm happy to have you lead this project."

"Listen, Greg," I said, "I may be assigned as your superior, but we're going to work together. I need you just as much as you need me."

We flew to Singapore and stayed for two weeks, working during the day and going out to the bars and clubs at night. Flush with the company card, we felt invincible. We expensed everything from drinks to dinners, and racked up quite a bill.

Back in the office, we were called into our boss's office and reprimanded for our extravagance. "You may be good engineers," our manager said, his words sharp and cold, "but you're lousy budgeters." He held up a page of expenses from our trip. "Never do this again."

This was the first time I'd been scolded by a boss in my life. I felt like a kid again caught playing in the street past curfew. I hate that feeling. If I was in a meeting with colleagues and we were arguing about a certain design idea, I would be bold in my assertions and push back against what I saw as shortsighted beliefs. But here, getting in trouble, I was mortified. "Never again," I told myself.

———·———

Chapter 16

~

During *my first year at FRH*, Harendra received his own visa to come work in the U.S. It was like old times—I gave him the spare room in my Rochelle Park apartment, and that first night, we talked about all the gossip back home and what he could expect from New York. He was shocked when I picked him up from the airport in my latest prized possession: a used Buick. "Big boss man," he joked and slapped my back. The car did make me feel like a boss. Often, I needed to get around this massive city, and public transportation, as I found out so well, could be faulty. Plus, I loved the freedom my car gave me. I'd take drives on the weekends out of the city, either up Long Island or down to the Jersey Shore. It was a thrill, but I knew it would be so much better if I had someone in the passenger seat with me.

When Harendra arrived, he didn't have a job lined up or a degree, but he was a hard worker and skilled negotiator. Just like me, he went from office to office, knocking on doors until he landed a job as a truck loader at a local warehouse. He worked between 7 p.m. and 2 a.m. He hated the job, but I reminded him: "Harendra. You can't be choosy. You have to start somewhere."

There wasn't an easy train or bus route to work, so I drove my brother to work and picked him back up every day. This meant I woke at 5 a.m., commuted to work at 6 a.m., got off work at 6 p.m., and drove him to work at 7 p.m., then I'd get four hours of sleep before having to pick him up at 2 a.m. I was happy when Harendra told me he was going to pick up overtime hours—that meant I got a little bit more sleep in the middle of the night.

It was hard, but I was still young and ready to support my brother to make as much money as possible.

One day, Harendra came home carrying a vacuum cleaner.

"What the hell is that for?" I asked.

"This is my future!" He laughed. "Ramesh, you won't believe it. I was out on a walk feeling sorry for myself and my lousy job when I ran into a salesman. We got to talking, and I found out he is the regional manager for Electrolux. He told me how they sell vacuums door to door, and for every machine he sells, he gets a commission. He gave me the job on the spot!"

"What?" I was shocked. "How are you going to do both jobs?" I asked.

"By not doing both jobs," he said, and smiled. "I quit the loading job just now."

"Wow," I said, "the pay must be pretty good for you to quit so fast."

"Well," Harendra started, then got shy.

"What?" I asked, getting worried.

"There are no wages."

"Brother, you're telling me you quit your salaried job to become a door-to-door salesman on commission?!"

"Yes!" he said, excited again. "But don't worry, Ramesh, I will make us both proud."

Those first few weeks, he failed to make us proud. In fact, he didn't sell one vacuum. I was worried—two men on one income is a tough road to travel, and if Harendra didn't make some deals, we'd be screwed.

Finally, I came home to Harendra and a pack of cold beer.

"What's all this?" I asked.

"You won't believe it."

"You sold a vacuum?"

"No. I sold five!"

"What!" I yelled. "How did you go from zero to five in one day?"

"Easy," Harendra said, popping open a beer and handing it to me. "I started going to the fancy neighborhoods where the rich white women live. Most of them are pretty old, and I started asking one of them what they hated about their vacuums. 'They're heavy,' they said. 'I hate lugging them up and down the stairs.' Then, a lightbulb went off in my head. I convinced them to buy two Electrolux vacuums to replace their one. That way, they could leave one on each floor." He also told me he convinced the women to buy enough supplies to never run out. He sold stacks of spare bags as a package deal.

That was the end of my anxiety of a one-income household. Harendra soon became one of the most popular salesmen and the top income producer in the tristate area. Not only that, but on one of his daily rounds, he met a young woman from Norway who worked as a housekeeper. After a string of dates, they got married and moved to a house in Yonkers.

I didn't see much of Harendra during those next few years. I was happy for his success and marriage, of course, but it left me lonely again. He'd call from time to time and give me updates: about his two beautiful daughters, or his eternal wanderlust for bigger and better jobs. At some point, he complained to his boss about how he makes more money than Harendra at Electrolux. They got in a fight, and my brother quit. Soon, he set up an import/export business for Indian fabrics. It was a tough time to deal with Indian suppliers in those days, and without electronic means of communication, supplies were notoriously unreliable. He lost money on that job and looked for another. Then, he turned to what he knew—our family heritage—and opened a retail sporting goods shop in the Bronx. From afar, I kept up with his struggles in business, but I wasn't much help since I had my own life to lead. Who knew that a decade later Harendra and I would be back at it, working together once again? Not me. At this point, I had something else on my mind. I wanted to find the love of my life.

———◆———

Chapter 17

$\mathbf{M}$*y routine was regular back then.* A bit too regular. Monday through Friday, I would work late, and my five-hour-a-day commute took up the rest of my time. Once I'd scrounged something together to eat, I was exhausted and in bed again. I didn't mind the "rat race," as they call it. I loved the work I was doing, and I was intent on learning new skills in my trade. This was my dream, after all. Once I went to Singapore and saw the world open before me—the possibilities of travel, and large-scale projects, of the way other engineers and managers loved to work with me—I realized how much I wanted to do this forever.

On the weekends, I would see my friends up in Harlem and crash on their floor. I'd roll up to their building and honk my horn three times, and they'd flock out to check out my car. One weekend, I arrived to find the guys already drinking. "A bit early, yeah?" I kidded.

"Ramesh, my man!" my friend yelled. "A classmate of ours is throwing a birthday party upstairs on the Gujarati floor."

"She's a hot chick, man," my other friend added, swigging his beer.

"Gujarati!" I laughed, and took the cigarette and beer handed to me. "You guys must be desperate."

"There's no denying Bihari girls are supreme," one of the guys said. "But Kalpana is as funny as she is foxy. Chug that beer, Casanova, and let's boogie."

"Is there gonna be food?" I asked, my stomach growling.

"A tableful of farsans, I bet," my friend said.

"Vegetarian it is then," I joked, hoping there'd be something more substantial than the usual Gujarati fare. We laughed and walked up the stairs to the upper floor where music flowed down the hall and out the open windows of the building. Young Indian men and women stood and talked and drank in the hallway. My friends said their hellos and introduced me around, and as I stepped in the apartment to grab some beers, I saw a girl in a leather miniskirt leaning against a sofa. She was gorgeous. I forgot about getting my friends drinks and picked up a beer, lit a cigarette, and tried to act cool.

"Not a bad party for a Gujarati," I said.

She smirked and looked me up and down.

"Not a bad face for a Punjabi," she tossed back, and I laughed.

The attraction was immediate. I don't remember talking to anyone else that night. Kalpana came from Baroda, the second largest city in Gujarat, and grew up in a strict, conservative family. There was no way she could get away with wearing an outfit like the one she was wearing back home, and she reveled in it. I could see the pleasure she got in showing off her slim figure. I couldn't stop staring.

"I wanted to be a nurse in England," she told me, "but my mother forbade it. So, I came to the U.S. instead. My uncle works at IBM and lives upstate. He helped me rent a room from his mother-in-law in the Bronx."

"I wanted to go to England too," I said. "That was my top choice. Then Canada. But the U.S. took me in."

"It's funny," she said. "My first choice was Australia. But here we are."

She looked in my eyes, and I felt buzzed—and not from the beer.

"Here we are," I repeated. I was mesmerized by her words. As I told her my story of the endless flights and missing bag, she frowned. "What's wrong?" I asked.

"People don't know how much emotional turmoil we go through. Just to get here and start from scratch. It's so difficult."

"But we're here, aren't we?" I said. "Listen. Music is playing. Beer is flowing. We've made it, Kalpana!" She allowed herself a small smile. "Can I call you sometime?" I asked.

"I don't have a telephone," she said, nonchalantly. "Anyway, I'm heading out of town soon." She made a move to walk away.

"Wait!" I said, a little too emphatically. She rolled her eyes, but smiled as I handed her a napkin with my phone number on it.

"If you have an opportunity," I said, "give me a call."

"Sure," she said, and walked off into the crowded room.

My heart was beating like a jackhammer. *That's it*, I thought. *She's the one.* Her personality was captivating, her sense of adventure alluring. *What a risk-taker*, I thought, *to travel from India to the U.S. alone. A single woman!*

After that party I thought of her every day. I didn't want to be alone anymore.

A few weeks went by when my phone rang.

"Ramesh," Kalpana said in her crystal-clear voice. "I'm back in the city. How have you been?"

We talked that evening for three hours. She told me she worked in lower Manhattan near 14th Street and offered to meet me there at 6 p.m.

the next day after she got off work. I was excited, but as luck would have it, my workload that day was grueling. A project wasn't going well, and I had to stay later than I thought. Running out of the office, I found myself in horrible traffic. By the time I got downtown, it was pushing past seven o'clock. I was ashamed, and I could tell Kalpana was slightly annoyed. I apologized profusely, and suggested we go for coffee at Chock Full o' Nuts. As we settled in, we began to talk. Hours passed without us noticing. It got late, and Kalpana excused herself—she had to wake early for work the next day. I asked if we could hang out tomorrow, and she agreed.

After that, we hung out every day. We didn't have much money, so we'd grab pizza and Coke and talk about our lives, our childhoods, and our dreams. Kalpana told me about the old apartment building she lived in. Her neighborhood was mostly Puerto Rican and dangerous. One night, she called me crying. She had been robbed walking home at sunset. I immediately invited her to move in with me in Roselle Park. She'd been there countless times, as I'd been to hers, and we both knew mine was a safer and quieter option.

We spent every weekend together, playing in the snow and taking the subway to new neighborhoods to walk and explore. We just wanted to spend as much time together as possible. Sometimes we'd drive upstate and rent a cabin or down to the Jersey Shore to swim in the sea. We took road trips to Niagara Falls, Toronto, and Montréal. We were young and carefree. Our love for each other was made sweeter by the fact that none of this—the sleepovers, the road trips . . . hell, even coffee at Chock Full O' Nuts—would have been possible back in India. She Gujarati, me Punjabi. Our love would have been forbidden before we could have said a single "hi" to each other.

But none of that mattered now when I held her in my arms and we talked about the future. My grand plans, her desire to start a family. The world felt very big then. Big enough to hold every dream we had and make them come true.

After some months, Kalpana urged us to marry, but I was hesitant. I was worried about what my family might say. "Let's wait another month," I told her, and then, a month later, "let's wait another month."

"Ramesh, please," she finally said. "Have you talked to your family yet?" Kalpana was much braver than I was. Even though her family was wary of our union, she told them she would marry me anyway, even if they didn't give their blessing. After some debate, her family agreed to support her. They said, "Do whatever you want; you're going to anyway."

I was still scared. I knew my siblings and mother wouldn't approve of a Punjabi marrying a Gujarati. I was worried what they might say, how they'd feel betrayed. I didn't want their guilt to push me down. I didn't want to house their regrets or see disappointment in their eyes.

"Please, Kalpana, be patient with me. It will happen." Anger flared in her eyes.

"If you have it your way," she said, "we'll be too old to start a family by the time we're married. How long do you expect me to wait?"

I hated to see disappointment in her eyes, but I just needed more time. After a few hours in another part of the apartment, Kalpana walked into the room to tell me she was going to London to stay with some friends and relatives. I was devastated, but I still didn't have to courage to resist my family's wishes.

After she left, my days became similar to when I was a bachelor. Wake, commute, work late, commute, eat, sleep, repeat. Day after day. Table tennis wasn't as fun anymore, and I was still awful at bowling. I felt distant from my coworkers as they drank beer and laughed at stupid jokes. I had to get Kalpana back.

"My love," I said to her on the phone, "will you marry me? I don't give a damn about anything else anymore except you."

"As long as you're serious, Ramesh, my answer is yes."

Kalpana returned to New York, and we got married in October. My family was, unsurprisingly, furious, so we didn't plan an event. Nor did we invite anyone. On a lunch break, Kalpana left the bank where she worked and I left my office, and we were officially married by the state at the courthouse—both of us in our regular work clothes. After we signed, we went back to work, and that was that. There was no celebration, no three-day wedding party or sumptuous feast. But we didn't need fancy clothes or dancing—you could see all the celebration we needed in our smiles.

We soon found a small apartment in Mineola on Long Island, where we lived for a year before buying a single-family house in Bedford. This house would become our base, our nest, for the next five years. As we finished unpacking our boxes, I stood in the doorway of our new home, looking at my wife. "Look at us," I said, beaming. "A Patna guy who fell in love with a Baroda girl."

"It's an impossible story," Kalpana said. And she hugged me.

An impossible story that could never happen in India. But it happened to me. It happened in New York City—a city where anything can happen.

———•———

Chapter 18

~

M*y superiors at Frederic R. Harris* appreciated my work in Singapore (despite the extravagant expenses) and sent me next to Halifax, a town in Nova Scotia, Canada. We were hired as part of a joint venture with Gulf Oil of Canada to plan and design the world's largest offshore terminal. My colleagues and I traveled to the site, inspected the terrain, and began drawing up plans. Gulf Oil gave me a beautiful two-bedroom apartment, and Kalpana visited several times over weekends when we'd drive into the countryside and explore the beautiful rolling green hills and rough Atlantic Ocean waves that crashed along the rocky beaches. It was delightful to learn about Canadian life and culture from the managing director of the company, with whom I became close friends. He'd invite me over for meals and we'd play table tennis over beers. At work, we'd brainstorm together about how to get this massive terminal to work. But no matter how much we chatted, swatted our paddles, and drew up designs, we couldn't figure out how to make it work. Gulf Oil of Canada abandoned the project as we were sent home.

It was tough returning home without finishing the project, but with every plan and design that didn't get made, I learned more and more about the craft of engineering and the complexities of the global trade of oil and gas. It fascinated me to think about extraction, storage, and transportation of this vital substance all over the world.

Soon, I was working on projects taking place in Turkey, Israel, and the U.S. I was regarded as a smart, intuitive, and hardworking engineer, and I was placed as a team lead on many projects. I made quite a name for myself in the industry in the '70s. Other companies heard about my talents, and I received offers for positions with them. Curious about potential opportunities, I took interviews at Fluor Corporation in Los Angeles, Bechtel Corporation in San Francisco, and Brown & Root in Houston, but I turned them all down. Fluor and Bechtel were too big and bureaucratic—they lacked the family atmosphere I loved at FRH. I didn't feel like I would have control over my own destiny at companies like that. I'd have to work in one of dozens of departments under someone else's command. I worried about having to answer to a superior I didn't know well. At FRH, I could take risks and break rules when they seemed counterintuitive to me, and even though I knew there might be a price to pay, the friendships I had with my colleagues in Manhattan assured me I'd get a fighting chance to explain my actions. At a place like Fluor, no way. I'd be out on the street with my first talk-back. I also rejected Brown & Root, but for a more personal reason; Houston was just too damn hot and humid.

These interviews reminded me how great my position was at FRH. That company gave me the freedom to develop new ideas without having to worry about being fired or promoted. I felt comfortable with the responsibilities I had, and I knew that, through my work, I had the power to make changes, however small, in the world around me. At the time,

I had no desire to one day run a company or be an executive. My only ambition was to someday manage a group of people involved in critical decision-making. I loved brainstorming for projects and working with intelligent people passionate about our work. There were, however, managers who weren't totally engaged and only cared about financial returns. I knew they were lacking an important piece of the puzzle in business: the overall impact on society of the work we were doing. That is just as, if not more, important than profit.

My next project at FRH was a massive, two-year commission: to design and build an offshore terminal in the Bahamas on Freeport Island. The terminal needed to handle large oil tankers, called supertankers, that would transport oil from the Middle East to Freeport. Then, at our new terminal, these supertankers would offload their oil into smaller tankers that could more easily navigate the ports along the eastern coast of the United States. This new terminal would reduce shipping costs and allow oil shipments to more ports along the coast.

On our first site visit, I was awed by the beauty of the waters in the Bahamas. The ocean was crystal clear, absolutely clean, with a visibility of a hundred feet. The beach sand was pure white, and the bright green palm trees that blew in the warm winds stood out against the bright blue sky. I felt an obligation that stretched deep into my bones that we had to protect this pristine environment no matter what. There would be no cutting corners, no cheap fixes. Everything we built had to be done with the utmost care for this island and these waters.

It was a challenge. The terminal had to stand two miles offshore in the middle of the water in order to receive the large supertankers at an adequate depth. Then, we had to build large pipelines that sunk into the sea deep enough to transport the oil to land without hampering the everyday routes of sea vessels in the area. We learned that we could weigh the pipes down by coating them in thick concrete so they would stay on the ocean floor, and the concrete had the added benefit of stabilizing the pipes so they wouldn't tear or leak.

The on-site project took eight months, and once we started to build, I was given a two-bedroom villa on the beach. Every day, I'd commute to the job site and work out of a makeshift trailer to oversee construction. Kalpana joined me for extended trips, and we'd suntan on my days off and go for midnight swims in the moonlight. The water and air were always warm and inviting, and we'd watch the sunset together and wonder how our friends were faring back in the tough New York winter. We were madly in love; I was enthralled by my work during the day and her beauty at night. On weekends, we'd jump over to Miami or Orlando for mini vacations.

A part of me wanted to stay on that beach with Kalpana forever, but we completed the project as planned and had to go back to New York. Once we settled back into our house on Long Island and saw old friends, I was happy to be back. And no sooner were we settled when Kalpana opened the door to me with a huge smile on her face and a palm on her stomach. She was pregnant. The Bahamas had blessed us with a little girl, who arrived in our arms in 1974. We called her Anita, and she became the Caribbean sun at the center of our lives.

———•———

Chapter 19

B*ack in the office, my boss approached me* with a new proposal. FRH had a joint venture with the Iranian National Oil Company designing mega-projects in the region. He asked me to act as the lead mechanical engineer to represent FRH during the design and buildout. The project was proposed to take twelve to eighteen months to complete, during which I'd live in Iran and work with local partners to complete the build. I immediately went home and talked to Kalpana about the proposal. The compensation was good and living and travel expenses were paid. Plus, I could take the whole family. Kalpana thought it would be a great adventure, so I eagerly accepted the offer, and we left our home in New York in the summer of 1975.

Tehran was a bustling, hospitable, and cosmopolitan city. We found a two-bedroom apartment in an uptown neighborhood where three- to four-story apartment buildings adjoined each other in long blocks. Our neighbors were like us, with most of them on assignment from the U.S., U.K., and other European countries. We quickly made friends, bought a car, and settled into our new life. We'd go out to dinner and have drinks at local bars and hang out at each other's houses. It was a social time—the workload for my project was surprisingly light. The city was liberal, and we never felt our freedoms curtailed in any way. Plus, Persians seemed to respect Indians—the Hindus, that is—because Iran was once part of the Indian subcontinent. There was a long history of trade between Indian and Persian cities for generations as merchants would cross the Arabian Sea in wooden ships. We all, as cheesy as it sounds, got along. It was simply a different time back then. Iran was a close ally of the United States and acted as a stabilizing force in the Middle East. The Iranian Air Force and Navy were equipped with top-grade U.S. weapons, and I met many Persian technicians who trained and went to university in the U.S. to become specialists back in Iran.

As the head of the mechanical engineering department at the Iranian National Oil Company, I was treated with respect. We had a handful of projects scattered around the country to oversee, and I'd take Kalpana and baby Anita with us on long drives around the country to sightsee, learn Persian customs, and buy souvenirs to take back home.

One day, I got a call that a man named K. was in the lobby and wanted to speak with me. He arrived in my office with an extended hand and large smile. He was a short man with dark features who lived in the United States and worked for a company called ATCO Rubber Products. He oversaw international sales for the company and was currently traveling the world for business. He pitched their latest product: a new type of duct recently developed by ATCO. It was a flexible duct made of polyester-encapsulated steel wire. I listened politely, taking a mental note of the pros and cons of the product, and then told him once his pitch was done, "Thank you for the information and opportunity, but I will not be purchasing your product because I have no use for it."

The duct was so new I had no idea how to determine its advantages. At that time, all ducting was made of sheet metal, which meant it had less chance of being a fire hazard and it was impermeable to damage during installation. With this new flexible polyester and steel wire duct, I had no idea how it felt, what it could withstand, or how fragile it might be to handle. K. was disappointed but left in good spirits.

The next day, K. invited me to dinner. "We're both Indian," he said, "and it's my last night in town. Let me take you out."

"Yes," I said, "but I live with my wife and daughter. Why don't you come over to my place?" K. was excited about a homecooked Indian meal, since he'd been living in the U.S. for a long time and didn't get the chance often to eat well. We talked about life in Iran, new business projects, and opportunities in the U.S. stock market.

A few months later, I received a letter from K. thanking me for my hospitality and then, toward the end, he offered me a job at ATCO. I was stunned. "We'd love to hire you as our International Sales Manager, taking over my role in sales around the world." I didn't know much about rubber, let alone this new product he was pushing. In the letter, K. enumerated the qualities he saw in me: smart, professional, clear-eyed about the future, and knowledgeable about business. I was flattered and humbled and I thanked him, but I respectfully declined. "I'm happy with my position at FRH. I get along with my colleagues. I'm not at a point where I see any reason to leave."

A few weeks later, K. wrote again, insisting I reconsider. "The position we are creating for you at ATCO is exceptional," he wrote, "and here, your future is bright. You have no choice but to say yes." But again, I said no.

Two more letters came and finally, to get him to stop, I said, "K., what about this? Once I'm back in New York City in December, I'll meet you and decide then."

He agreed, but fate would have him wait another year. Management was so happy with my work that they asked me to extend my stay in Tehran. It was such a good deal that I accepted immediately. Kalpana and Anita went back to Bedford while I spent another year in Tehran. I forgot about K. and ATCO and flexible ducts and continued my tenure in the Middle East, busying myself until my return to New York to be with my family again.

When I did return to Bedford in 1977, I was surprised to find a letter from K. reminding me of my promise to meet with him.

"This man is relentless," I told Kalpana.

"Just go meet with him and be done with it," she said.

So, I called his number. K. practically jumped for joy at my voice. He immediately arranged a flight for me to visit him in Michigan. Hanging up, I sat down with Kalpana and told her the news.

"Before you go," she said, "let's discuss the pros and cons."

"If I worked at ATCO, I would enter into a completely new line of work. At FRH, I have upward mobility; my bosses love me and respect me; I feel taken care of. What do I know about sales, or rubber products?"

"Look at Harendra," she said. "Look at your father. Sales is in your blood. Just keep an open mind, listen to what they have to say, and you can decide then. I support you whatever you decide to choose."

I smiled at Kalpana, feeling lucky to have her as my confidante and wise advisor.

"Thank you, my love," I said, and went into the bedroom to pack.

———◦———

Chapter 20

~

The flight to Grand Haven, Michigan was short and uneventful. The town itself sounded a bit boring—I'd never heard of it before. Did I really want to move to a new state in a completely new area of the country where I knew no one? K. had better offer me a lucrative deal to take me away from the comfort of my job and friends in New York.

The town was located on the western side of Michigan, a sleepy little town adjacent to Grand Rapids and close to another small town called Holland. Back then, the largest industry in Michigan was the automotive industry, with big and small car companies scattered throughout the state. So, ATCO was a bit of an anomaly, working as they did in rubber products.

I met K. at a restaurant for lunch. He was accompanied by the owner of ATCO named Charles Anderson. "Call me Chuck," he said with a big handshake and a smile. Our chat was genial and flowed smoothly. We talked about my trips abroad and the oil terminals I'd worked on. We also chatted about one of my favorite topics: the stock market and investment opportunities. Chuck asked how I got involved in stocks.

"I've always been in awe of the U.S. stock market, and the first thing I vowed to do when I got a job in this country was buy stocks. One day, while working for Mr. Gardner, a mutual fund broker came to the office. He gave me a big pitch and guaranteed me X amount of money if I invested. I said yes, completely believing him. I didn't ask questions. I didn't have much money either, so it seemed like a small risk. I just wanted to get my feet wet, see what happens."

"What did happen?" Chuck asked.

"I lost it all." We all laughed. "It wasn't much, like fifty dollars a month, but it taught me how to be smarter with investing. I've been in the stock market ever since."

"And are you still losing money?"

"No, in fact, here is my philosophy," I told them. "People think buying stock is gambling. It's not. It's simply about making products. It's about putting your money behind a product that will be successful. People go on and on about a good market or a bad market and when to invest. None of that matters. Nor is there any luck in stocks either. That's another myth."

"That's not what I've been told," K. said. "It seems like there's a lot of luck involved. It's just another form of gambling."

"No, I disagree," I said. "It's not gambling at all. Stocks have patterns. Look, I don't care how great a stock has done, but if it goes below twenty percent of its value, I sell. No matter what. People get emotional, thinking it'll rise back up. And maybe it will. But that's not smart investing."

The two men listened to what I had to say: K. with skepticism, Chuck with enthusiasm.

"Always, always minimize downside risk, and allow unlimited upsize. This is how to make money in stocks, and this is how you run a good business."

Chuck shook his head. As he took out his wallet to pay the bill, he turned to me and said, "Ramesh, I've met hundreds of people around the world. But you are the smartest man I've ever met. Your travel experience, your insights into global trade, finances, engineering. Hell, you know more than K.!" I felt bad for K., but he laughed with us and took it well.

On the flight back home, I went over our conversation again and again. My gut told me to reject the offer. I had no experience in flexible ducting for air conditioning systems, they worked out of a small factory in Grand Haven, they only employed forty people, and the building was small and poorly ventilated. I felt like I would be a failure. On top of all that, the two owners of the company, Chuck and his partner Bill Tuggle, had completely different objectives in life. Chuck was an ambitious engineer who dreamed about expanding ATCO to become a national brand. Bill, however, was a laid-back engineer who, although smart and creative, wanted to keep operations small so he could retire in Michigan without much fuss. It seemed unwise to walk into that can of worms. Business partnerships are like a marriage; if two people have different visions of the future, you're bound to end up with neither.

The next day at work, I explained my trip to my colleagues. Everyone agreed with me; leaving Frederic R. Harris would be a big mistake. My managers were already drawing up plans for me to move to Saudi Arabia and after that, Egypt. "Think of all the countries you'll visit if you stay here," one of my coworkers said. "You've got it made."

But my home life gave me a different perspective. My daughter was now two and a half years old, and Kalpana was ready for some stability. I didn't blame her. Carting your toddler around the Middle East wasn't exactly the upbringing we'd imagined for our child. "Plus," Kalpana said, "who knows what kind of schools they have over there? And how is she supposed to make any lasting friendships?"

Of course, my wife was right. Jumping from country to country was fun when you're single or young and newly married, but it's not ideal while raising a family.

Just then, we heard loud knocks on our door and the voice of our relatives yelling for us to open up already. "That said," she continued with a bit of mischief in her eyes, "getting away from New York could be nice." We were lucky to have relatives nearby to help with childcare and gather for holidays, but many of them still held the old Indian mentality of visiting at odd times without any notice and with the expectation that we would treat them like royalty. Lately, it felt like a tug-of-war between our desire to have peace and quiet and our family's desire to barge in at any moment with the latest gossip and endless complaints about cousins and siblings and ungrateful children.

That night, as Kalpana put some leftovers on the stove and served tea, I began to think that Grand Haven might not be so bad after all.

———◦———

Chapter 21

It was decided. I was going to take another massive risk, one that would upend my future, take me away from my friends, and plop me down in a new town, in a new state, to work with strangers, with no surety of financial gain and zero guarantee of success. I was going to take the job at ATCO—an unproven company with an indiscernible future. What was I thinking?

"Follow your heart," my superior manager at FRH had finally told me when I asked him what to do. "It's obviously been on your mind for months. Sure, it's a risk. But you'll never know until you try it out and see. Plus," he continued, "you can always come back here."

"Thank you," I said and prepared to tell Kalpana I'd finally made my decision. Luckily, K. and Chuck were in no rush to have me join them

> **CALCULATED RISK #2:**
>
> Moving to a new
>
> industry with no
>
> guarantee of success.

right away. It would take some time for me to pack up and sell my house and move to Michigan. They didn't even have a position for me! The plan of being the international sales manager didn't fit my skillset, so Chuck decided to create a new role for me at the company called "Manager of Special Projects," which meant they had no special projects and would need to invent some, and fast. In the meantime, I was tasked to learn about the rubber and ducting industry, research ATCO's competitors, and dig into growth possibilities. Then, I'd fly out to Michigan every few weeks to chat about potential projects until we finally settled in Grand Haven, our new home. During these trips, I stayed in a Holiday Inn in a town called Springtown about five miles from Grand Haven. Everyone who worked there was kind to me. No one ever treated me differently because I was Indian, which was a bit of a surprise. In Manhattan, there are so many cultures piled on top of each other that people are used to diversity. However, I'd heard that the Midwest could be different, a bit more xenophobic. But I didn't experience that at all.

During one early trip to Michigan, I was caught in the most violent snowstorm in the state's history. My hotel guests and I were stranded in the hotel for three days, and management took great care of us. They used snowmobiles to shuttle food and supplies to us from local shops. We were all glued to the TV to see when the storm would pass. *Another snowy city*, I thought, *and this one is even worse than in New York!* But even this rough weather didn't deter me from wanting to work for ATCO. It actually seemed like a good omen—a sign that I was doing something right.

To my relief, while still in New York, Chuck told me that he and Bill Tuggle were splitting up. Amicably, of course, but they kept me insulated from their negotiations. I'm not sure what the final outcome was with their deal together, but the general idea was to split ATCO in two; Ramesh would stay with the present company headed by Chuck and K., with K. being appointed general manager and Chuck as owner and president.

Our first major goal was to find a new headquarters for our new ATCO company. I began poring over state maps to find possible sites for our factory and office. First, I figured out where most of our business already took place. Then, I asked Chuck for a list of his personal preferences. Chuck wanted to relocate to the West Coast. He loved Lake Tahoe, and his daughter was going to school in Los Angeles. I, however, saw that most of our distribution and sales took place in the Southeast. Plus, L.A. was insanely expensive. I also wanted a city with easy access to air travel as well as future growth potential. Without telling Chuck, I focused on Orlando, Atlanta, and Dallas. With a protractor, I drew a three-hundred-mile radius circle around each city and looked at the towns nearby. I looked at local wages, taxes, ease of business permits, availability of suitable real estate, and the friendliness of the local people. In the end, Atlanta was okay, but it was a long flight to California. Orlando was too hot and muggy. My eyes lit up at Dallas. They just finished a state-of-the-art international airport in 1973 with the added benefit of allowing us to travel to any part of the U.S. in three hours or fewer. I wasn't excited about the heat down there, but otherwise, I thought it would be perfect.

I prepped a book with these factors listed as pros and cons along with my final analysis. My managers were impressed with my work and quickly agreed. Chuck grumbled. He still had his mind set on California, but after double-checking my work, he knew I was right. Dallas it was.

Next, I had to find a site near Dallas for ATCO. Equipped with the criteria of the building we would need, I contacted the Chambers of Commerce in the towns scattered around Dallas.

"How many employees do you have?" they asked.

"Around forty," I said, and I immediately got the cold shoulder.

"Oh, I see, sure, sure. Here are some real estate firms you can contact," and I never heard from them again. They weren't warm or inviting, and I suspected they weren't too keen to work with an Indian immigrant, even though I'd been in the U.S. for nearly a decade by this point. Luckily, the real estate agent they connected me to was kind and encouraging. He and I became quick friends, and we planned a trip for him to show me properties around the city.

I flew to Dallas right before one of the worst snowstorms in city history. Now, all I could do was chuckle, since huge piles of snow outside my window always happened when I was starting a new venture. And the first three turned out great.

Once the snow stopped falling and the roads were clear, I toured buildings in Dallas, Arlington, and Grand Prairie. But none of them were all that great. Plus, they were way overpriced, and everyone treated me with a bit of disdain. They weren't going to put any effort into a company unless they had over a thousand employees. I got the feeling I was a waste of their time, which isn't a good way to start any business deal.

On the third day, another snowstorm hit the area, and business and transportation shut down completely. Stuck in my hotel room, I took out my map and began searching around Dallas one more time. I came across a small town called Fort Worth. It looked intriguing. I called their Chamber of Commerce, which was technically closed due to the storm, but a representative answered the phone and excitedly listened to me talk about ATCO and our plans. They arranged a meeting for me the next day with the town's economic development manager, named Jim Wells, and their chairman. You'd think they'd never had a company interested in relocating to Fort Worth before! They pulled out the red carpet treatment for me. It was the exact opposite from my reception in

Dallas. For Fort Worth, a company of forty employees was a big catch, and I was ready to be reeled in.

We met downtown and they showed me a film about the history of Fort Worth, its growth over the decades, and facilities they provided to businesses looking to relocate there. Afterward, a real estate agent gave a presentation and took me on a tour of the city, showing me important monuments and buildings and vacant real estate available to rent or buy on short notice. Jim Wells promised to collect more information regarding the questions I had and send it my way by the next week.

I have to say, I was quite impressed. I liked the city's laid-back atmosphere. It didn't take itself too seriously. And everyone was super friendly. I went back to Michigan with rave reviews to Kalpana and my coworkers. Unsurprisingly, no one had ever heard of the place. I began to wonder if this might be a hard sell to Chuck.

In a few days, I received a huge package from Jim containing detailed reports of Fort Worth's economic growth, newly relocated businesses, wage scales, and labor pool viability. For the next four hours, I pored over the data. The small town fit everything ATCO needed, and Kalpana and I agreed on one property that looked just perfect.

I called Jim and flew down to meet him again to look at the site. He took me to other possible buildings for rent, but my mind was set on the first one. "What kind of deal are you looking for?" I asked Jim, and we sat down and went over all the details. By this point, with my work at FRH and Gardner, I felt confident in my skills as a negotiator. I channeled the wisdom of my father and brother and sat looking at Jim and the real estate agent with a mission: to get the lowest, best possible price I could. We went back and forth several times until the agent agreed to my terms: low rent for five years, after which I had the option to buy. Jim was shocked, but he warned he needed to get the property owner's approval before moving forward with the deal. "Sure," I said. "I also need to get approval from my team and boss, Mr. Anderson, before I can sign anything."

I returned to my hotel room and called K. "Fly down here ASAP!" I yelled, excited for my bosses to see what I'd been able to accomplish in such a short time. When they landed, I took them to dinner, laying out maps of Fort Worth and a detailed schematic of the property. Instead of a bright smile, Chuck scowled.

"What the hell is all this, Ramesh?" he asked. A dark cloud formed over my head. "I thought you said you were looking in Dallas. This," he pointed to Fort Worth, a small dot far from Dallas's city center, "is some tiny town I've never heard of."

"Chuck, please," I said, "hear me out. It's got great growth potential, and—"

"No!" he yelled. "I already compromised on Los Angeles. We agreed to move to Dallas. Now you're trying to take us to Fort Worth. I can't accept that."

"The cities are very close together," I pleaded.

"Who even told you to go to Fort Worth?" He was fuming.

"I've done the research, Chuck. Fort Worth will save us a ton of overhead. It's a much better place."

"No. I want Dallas."

"But it's more expensive, and the labor market is worse, and wages are higher . . ."

"I don't care," he yelled. "I want Dallas, or else this trip is an entire waste of my time."

"Fine!" I yelled back, finally losing my temper. I threw down my napkin and pen. "It's your money, Chuck. Do whatever you want with it. I'm out of here." I stood up to leave. "I don't want to work for someone who wants to throw their money down the drain."

"Okay, okay," Chuck said, holding his hands up to calm me down. "Ramesh, sit. Let's talk about it tomorrow and finish our meal. We don't want to let our food go to waste too."

"Fine," I said, sitting down. I was still too hot to eat. "Look, Chuck, this is all I'll say. I did the research. I believe in my work. It's your money, and you're free to blow it however you want. But if you decide to choose Dallas, I'm walking."

He was shocked by my outburst, but he kept his composure. Later, he told me that he never had a new employee stand up to him like that or disagree with him so vehemently. He could tell I was unwavering in my convictions, and although he wasn't getting what he wanted, he had to admit I was putting the interest of the company above everything else, including personal desires. I mean, I wasn't super-excited to relocate my family to a tiny town in Texas, but if that's what the numbers said would make us succeed, then that's what we had to do. It was clear, common sense. And Chuck just couldn't quite see it—yet.

We ended the meal without me touching my plate with a plan to meet again the next day. I was confident in what I had said and regretted nothing, but that night, I did wonder if I was going to lose my job over this. My inner voice kept saying, *You can't let them make a wrong decision. It's your responsibility to fight over this.*

Luckily, Chuck was in a cheerful mood the next morning, and I offered to take him on a tour of Dallas. I showed him each building Jim offered me, explained the layout of the city, and described the labor pool available to them. I could see him eyeing the old buildings, the poor quality of sites, and the fact that anything decent was far from downtown. The one building he admitted could work would have to be divided into two parts, one for offices and one for research and development. The cost, when we discussed it, would be exorbitant and impractical.

"Now," I said, his face a bit crestfallen, "let's check out Fort Worth."

Chuck and K. marveled at the drive. The open space, the wide freeways, and the easy access and zero traffic enthralled them. I took them to each building I'd rejected, explaining my process of elimination. Then, I took them to the pièce de résistance, the building I had already (without them knowing) negotiated a deal to lease. They marveled at the two-story, single-occupancy building with room for expansion. They saw how it was in an industrial park next to beautiful fountains and tons of parking for employees. It was then I told them the lease I had already brokered, starting with months of free rent, then below-market rent for five years with the option to buy. Chuck and K. were visibly impressed.

"I have to admit," Chuck said, "this place is a perfect size for the needs of our office and research facility. But it still needs work inside to make it suitable."

"Of course, Chuck. I've already thought of that, and here is the name of a highly qualified general contractor who has already agreed to renovate the building to our specifications . . ."

We kept chatting as we drove to a local restaurant, and now Chuck and K. were listing the advantages of Fort Worth in relation to Dallas. Chuck finally relented and gave his approval.

"Contact the real estate agent and set up a meeting for tomorrow so we can sign the papers," he said. That night, I ate my entire meal, plate licked clean, plus dessert.

———•———

Chapter 22

～

For the next three months, I felt like I was living inside a tornado. After the papers were signed, Chuck put me in charge of prepping the site for occupancy. I hired the general contractor, who brought on a team of subcontractors. They renovated the electrical and plumbing systems, built new bathrooms, and partitioned the office space into private rooms. I set aside two large rooms for executive suites for Chuck and K., and upstairs, I put a large meeting room that opened onto a large patio for outdoor conferences. As the buildout got underway, managers would visit from Michigan and offer suggestions and ideas to meet their specific needs. I kept a live document listing these optimization points and shared them with the contractor.

It was exhilarating. There's nothing like building out an office space from scratch. You get to help optimize workflow by floorplan and create space for conversation, for brainstorming, for private digging-your-heels-in work. And I found I was quite good at it.

The next big chunk of my energy went into relocating ATCO's massive data processing equipment from Michigan. This was 1977, so we didn't have high-efficiency computers that could fit neatly on a desk. These were big machines that needed temperature control so they wouldn't overheat and short-circuit. I decided to build a raised pedestal in one of the rooms so that, when the equipment sat on top of it, we could run cool air below plus allow space to hide necessary electrical infrastructure. With the help of my team, we figured out these logistics in no time.

For weeks, I could be found sitting on the floor in one of the office spaces as I researched and contacted vendors to find the most efficient and cheapest workers to get our building ready for action. One day, Chuck came to show the site to his wife.

"What are you doing sitting on the floor?" he asked as he entered the room.

"I'm looking for a good deal on chairs and tables, but I haven't found it yet."

"That's Ramesh in a nutshell," he said and laughed. "You see why I had to hire this guy?" he asked his wife. "He spends company money just like it's his own. Which means, he's always looking for a way to save a buck. You don't find that level of frugality in workers these days."

I then told them about my extravagant trip to Singapore when I was just starting out at Frederick R. Harris and how embarrassed I was in getting reprimanded.

"Never again," I told Chuck and his wife. "I'll happily sit on the floor until I can find us good comfortable chairs at a decent price!"

Chuck beamed. For the owner of a company, employing a fiscally responsible worker is worth his weight in gold. Sometimes, quite literally.

That first year was a turbulent one for ATCO. Most managers made the move to Texas, but some decided to stay put up north, so we went

on a hiring spree to fill vacancies with local talent. Some of those workers from Michigan couldn't stand the Texas heat and quit by year end.
We were constantly trying to stabilize our staff, and the continued flow
of people coming and going added a level of stress none of us cared to
acknowledge. We just put our noses to the grindstone and pushed through.

And push through we did. By 1978, ATCO's little kingdom included
our corporate office in Fort Worth and two operation plants, one in
Grand Haven, Michigan and the other in Springdale, Arkansas. While
Chuck and K. managed the entire company, I handled the day-to-day
management of the office and personnel. Soon, I had to deal with more
than just complaints from employees about the Texas summer sun.
There was something else more oppressive exhausting my coworkers,
and his name was K.

K. had a business background. He received an MBA from the
University of Michigan in Ann Arbor, and Chuck had total faith in his
abilities. As ATCO's GM, he had full control of the company, which
included operations, sales, marketing, and finance. We all reported to
him. While he was a smart businessman, he was less talented in managing
people. He wasn't an encouraging boss, nor could he discern someone's
talents and help utilize them to the best of their ability. Plus, he came
across as arrogant, and with his GM credentials, he felt he had immunity
to do whatever he felt like doing. I remember one day disagreeing with
a decision K. made and bringing it up with Chuck.

"Whatever K. says goes," Chuck said, and ended the conversation
then and there.

Chuck was enamored with K., it was clear, and this I knew was a
big mistake. Just like love can blind you to another person's faults, so
too can professional naiveté. I began to hear stories from my coworkers
and see the way K. dealt with employees. He didn't tolerate mistakes

of any kind and was quick to terminate any worker for a small error. Most other managers couldn't stand his temperament but were afraid to voice their opinions because they might lose their jobs. He was a bit of a tyrant, this fellow Indian businessman, and I knew we were headed toward disaster.

On top of his lack of people skills, he wasn't all that great at finances either. He struggled to control expenses commensurate with revenue. After a few months in Fort Worth, I began to see us lose money in operations. Performance deteriorated that first year, and each quarter brought another round of losses. Low morale stalked the office hallways like a plague. Managers jumped ship at any comparable offer from another company. We all worked with our heads down, fearing a dark future, and the grumblings continued. Every few months, I'd get a call from my old manager at Frederic R. Harris, begging me to come back. "Your old position is waiting for you," he'd say. "Come warm up your old chair and work with us again. You had your little adventure, and it's time to come back to the big boys." I'd thank him and say, "Not yet. But also, not no. I'll keep you posted."

Chuck observed our company's struggles from afar, but he never once intervened. This frustrated me to no end. How can a boss of a company allow for this kind of failure? The warning signs were there in lost workers and lost revenue. What else did he need to happen to make a change?

I called Chuck in for a private meeting.

"Sir, do you know what's going on here?" I pleaded with him.

"Things are a bit rocky, yeah, but with our relocation and unstable workforce, it's bound to cause some ripples. It'll even out soon enough."

"No offense, Chuck," I said, "but you're delusional if you think doing nothing will right this sinking ship. If conditions here don't improve, most of your managers—including myself—will be out of here."

"You can't be serious, Ramesh," he said. "Just have some patience and faith."

"I don't need faith to show me what's going on around here," I told him. "And if this is how you want to run your company, I wish you all the best. But I'm going to find work somewhere that cares about making a profit."

"No, no, no. Ramesh, please. Stay. Give me a few months to figure this all out. I'll make improvements. Just stick with me for a bit until I do."

I didn't have much faith in Chuck at that point, but I considered his offer and agreed to ride out the next three months to see what he could do. I returned to my colleagues and told them about the meeting. We got back to work, still with our heads down, but allowing a glimmer of hope to shine on the periphery.

———◆———

Chapter 23

⁓

Of course, I couldn't just twiddle my thumbs while the company sailed into a sea of utter ruin. I didn't leave my home in Patna halfway across the world to become a failure ten years later. So, I went back to one of my strongest and most reliable friends in a time of need: education. I enjoyed the work at ATCO, which was far removed from the engineering work building oil terminals of my youth. I decided I should strengthen my knowledge and expertise in business, especially management. My undergraduate degree in mechanical engineering from India wouldn't be of much use with my new dream of rising through the executive ranks to take on larger and larger management roles. So, for self-improvement—and a solid distraction from the unhappiness at work—I enrolled in an MBA program at the University in Arlington, a city outside of Dallas. ATCO, to my surprise, helped with the tuition fees. Chuck really did want me to stay, didn't he? I worked during the day and attended classes at night, with Kalpana supporting me and running our home throughout it all.

Unfortunately, the caliber of teaching at the university was . . . less than enthralling, and I quickly lost interest. A friend told me to investigate the University of Dallas, which had a better reputation, was private, and employed teachers with practical, in-office experience. For example, the finance professor was a CFO of a local company who intimately knew the challenges facing a manufacturing company in Texas. This program was as tough as the first one was easy. My professors challenged me more than anything I'd ever done—even engineering school! I learned the practicalities of business law, marketing, finance, and HR, which I then brought to ATCO's office the next day. It was exhilarating to enact my newfound knowledge from school to actual problems needing swift solutions at work. With Kalpana's support, I worked hard and studied hard and graduated with top honors.

Soon after graduating, I learned, confidentially, that K. had made a deal with Chuck to buy the company and run it himself. This perturbed me, but when he approached me and told me the news himself, he asked if I would join him, and I said yes. Even though I didn't have much confidence in him, I believed in the team he assembled around him to make the right decisions for the company.

But the dark cloud in the office didn't dissipate. Managers were still caught within day-to-day confusion and weekly chaos. We all were just waiting for the other shoe to drop—a deeply negative profits report that would send us all packing. K. admitted to me that he decided to pull out from buying the company. He didn't have the capital to purchase ATCO, and I could tell his confidence had been shaken to its foundation, and he had no clear plan for ATCO's future. You could see how such poor leadership affects every employee in a company. And, with my new business savvy skillset, I realized this was the last straw.

"I'm putting in a three-month notice," I told Chuck. "I just can't do this anymore. K. is still running this company into the ground, and soon, there's no chance of us turning it around again." Chuck panicked.

"Ramesh, come on. K. is a smart guy. We're just going through some growing pains. He knows what he's doing."

"Like hell he does!" I yelled. "He has zero vision for this company."

"Oh, and you do?" Chuck asked.

"More than K. He'd be happy to be a regional leader in flexible ducting," and I scoffed.

"And what would make you happy?"

"The only thing that would make me happy is ATCO becoming a global leader in flexible ducting."

Chuck was silent.

"Okay, Ramesh," he said finally. "I'll think about what you said."

"If you don't," I said, "I'm done."

K. left that week on a one-month holiday, and while he was gone, Chuck and I put our heads together to create a new strategic plan without K. My boss secretly promoted me to vice president, which I kept secret from my colleagues as we began to right all the wrongs K. had done.

When K. returned, Chuck called him in for a three-day closed-door meeting to explain his new strategic plan: Chuck would take over sales and marketing, I would oversee purchasing, data processing, and operations, and K. would manage finances—as a consultant for one year. Once that year was up, he would be let go with a generous severance package.

I was elated. Finally, the obstacle of K. had been lifted from my path, and I now had a more direct line of authority between Chuck and me. K. took it well. And, as the weeks passed, my colleagues began to joke around in the breakroom again and a few smiles emerged throughout the day. It was like we finally felt the sun on our faces after a long winter storm.

Energized by the shift in management, I told Chuck flat-out that with the added responsibilities on my plate, and as vice president, I should have some ownership of the company. "Sure," he said, "but do you have the cash to buy shares?"

I didn't. But I knew it was important to have shares of the company I was about to throw my whole life into—because I had a vision. I saw ATCO becoming the biggest flexible ducting manufacturer in the world. And I wanted a share of that company immediately to secure my future fortune: for myself, Kalpana, and my children. Yes, plural; Kalpana and I had our second child, Niraj, in 1978, completing our family with a smiling ball of boyish joy.

I went to the bank to take out a loan, but they needed a guarantee: some collateral I didn't have.

"Kalpana, what should I do?" I asked when I got home. She was bouncing Niraj on one knee while combing Anita's hair on the other.

"Well, you do have one asset you could use as collateral," she said.

I looked around me at our house, full of photographs from our trips abroad, furniture we chose together to make a home, and my two young kids.

"Are you sure?" I asked.

"Are you sure," she asked back, "that you can do what you say you're going to do with ATCO?"

"Yes," I replied.

"Then do it," she said. "Something inside me tells me this is the right choice. I have total faith in you." I hugged her and the kids. "Look," she went on, "we're young enough to take some punches if they come. I do worry about them," she nodded to the children, "but tomorrow, if this whole thing blows up in our faces and we lose our house, we can get other jobs. We can manage."

I then took the third biggest risk in my life; I signed over my house as collateral to secure a bank loan to buy 10 percent of ATCO, a company that, up until then, was losing money. If my plan failed and ATCO failed, I'd be flat broke. But I felt, deep down, this would all

CALCULATED RISK #3:

Put up my house and assets as collateral to buy a company operating at a loss.

pay off. I had a vision. I also had a new monthly bill to pay, and I knew I had to work hard to earn enough money to pay off the loan and become debt-free. There was a fire under my ass, and I needed to make moves. And no one now could stand in my way.

———◦———

Chapter 24

~

It *was 1984. I owned a tenth of ATCO.* I had two beautiful children, I was blessed with a supportive and brilliant wife, and Chuck made me general manager of his company—or rather, our company. "You're in charge now," he said. "Do whatever you want."

Each time ATCO made a profit, I was able to buy more and more shares of the company. I couldn't wait to spring into action and make ATCO as profitable as possible. Once K. was gone, I immediately put my strategic plan into action. We restructured the company, and with K. gone, morale and performance improved. My colleagues were happy to see me take on a bigger role in the office. Also, since I'm tight with the purse strings, I reined in expenses, and our next quarter we made a profit again. Chuck and I became very close at this point. We'd meet at the local Denny's restaurant and chalk out future courses of action for the company. I reduced costs in purchasing and operations and improved supply chain management. The machine began to run with optimized efficiency, and ATCO was full steam ahead.

It was during this period when I implemented the first of three major changes at ATCO that influenced our entire industry.

The first was a problem of inventory. Our warehouse in Fort Worth was always full of materials and finished products. The plant manager told me it had to do with payment terms. "Because of the way we bill clients, we can't ship product before the 25th of each month. We build, build, build and then ship it all on the 26th." I was dumbfounded. All this inventory, which took up space and decreased our manufacturing capacity, was sitting there for no reason other than how an invoice was filled out?

"Please explain this to me," I said.

"Well, the industry works on a payment plan called '2 percent net 10th prox 10.'"

"What the hell does that mean?" I asked.

"'Prox' is short for 'proximo mense,' Latin for 'next month.' So, let's say you're a customer and you need ducting at a site starting in June. If the product is shipped on the 24th of May, you'll receive it before June 1st, and your bill is due on or before July 1st with a 2 percent discount. However, if the product is shipped on the 25th or later, you'll receive it after June 1st, which means you don't have to pay till July 10th with a 2 percent discount. You're given an extra ten days before your payment is due."

"What does all that matter to us?" I asked.

"It matters when a company needs cash to meet specific financial goals, such as payroll on the 15th, let's say. With 2 percent net 10th prox 10, we make sure we're flush to pay out expanses. And since our finances have been a bit . . . in the red since the relocation here, we stick to this plan."

"And end up with a crowded warehouse full of products that could ship but aren't because we're on a razor-thin wire with expenses. Doesn't that seem like a tightrope act, balancing just so we don't fall and kill ourselves? Look! All these boxes are just blocking our capacity to manufacture more products that we could sell to increase profits. If we stick with this system, we'll never scale to a size greater than we are now."

Around me, the warehouse was full of products waiting to be shipped for another week. And for no other reason than a strange billing code that everyone seemed to follow. On the 26th and 27th of the month, trucks would line up to be loaded, but because the shipments were so massive, we ran out of workers to load them. Those days were the most stressful for everyone in the factory, while the week before everyone was practically sitting on their hands with nothing to do. That wave of no work, then five days of chaos, then no work made no sense.

"Chuck," I said at Denny's that Friday, "this is ridiculous. We need to change this stupid system."

"Nah," Chuck said. "We can't. It's an industry standard."

"But why?" I asked, exasperated.

"This is how it's done, Ramesh. We've been operating like this for twenty years. Who are we to change that? Don't fix what isn't broken. You might just create a disaster."

I pushed around my food and grumbled. "I can't accept that explanation," I said. "I'm going to look into it."

The next week, I locked myself in my office to study the problem. This system felt lazy to me. I felt like an outsider learning a new language, but the language was cumbersome and hard to follow. I knew something needed to change. Traditions must be broken when they get in the way of good business. And good business is about making money—not following old-school rules based on nothing but wanting to be flush with cash for one day just to barely pay employees. If you're worried about having enough cash on hand for payroll, you've got deeper problems.

No, that explanation didn't cut it.

After a few days, I came up with a payment plan that would allow us to ship any time of the month. Chuck was anxious, and we argued about implementing my plan.

"We may lose everything!" he finally moaned.

"We have to take this risk," I said. "The payoff is beyond measure."

"I just don't see it, Ramesh."

"Don't worry," I said, a confident smile on my face. "You're not going to lose."

It was a massive success; within three months, all our competitors copied ATCO's new billing and shipping system. Our warehouse was always half-empty, with ample room for unexpected large orders and streamlined manufacturing. Trucks rolled in and out of the loading dock with ample workers to fill them. If an order was finished on the 10th, it shipped on the 10th instead of sitting around for two more weeks. Chuck was thrilled.

"I never would have made that change if you hadn't forced it on me," he admitted at Denny's. "I was scared."

"I know you were," I said. "But look; we've set a new industry standard now. And I bet we'll see its effect on profits soon enough."

And soon enough, we did.

———•———

Chapter 25

Profits *were rising*, and with each profitable quarter, we began opening new plants around the Eastern region of the country. We now had factories humming along in Springdale, Indiana; Fort Worth, Texas; Tampa, Florida; Greensboro, North Carolina; and Harrisburg, Pennsylvania. With every new plant we opened, I would manage operations, cut costs, and streamline customer experience. I saw that every new opening allowed us to better serve our customers while cutting transportation time as well. It was a win/win situation.

Our sales were good, but I could tell we would hit a wall with growth in a few years, and we needed to get inventive. Around that time, Chuck invited me to travel with him to trade shows to meet people in the field and gain more hands-on experience about business and marketing. I could see, after a few shows, how competitive our industry was. As we took notes and chatted, Chuck and I saw that our growth potential was marginal at best. I remember at one trade show we learned that one of our close competitors, Clecon, was considering selling their company.

"They're part of a large British group," Chuck said off the cuff. "They're not doing well. I don't see much potential in their business, though. Nor do they seem like a threat. ATCO is small, but at least we're nimble."

This offhanded comment stuck with me for a long time. I actually *could* see problems we were having specifically because of this competitor. I finally told Chuck we should look into the sale.

"No," he said, "we can't afford it. Anyway, we don't have the management skills to run two companies."

I listened to his words and nodded, knowing that Chuck had a better understanding about this area of business, but something gnawed at me. Buying this company just *felt right*. The idea of subsuming this company (and their assets) under the ATCO brand was exciting. Think of the synergy of such an acquisition! Plus, ATCO could capitalize on the market position by getting rid of this direct competitor. It made so much sense to me. But, still, I didn't want to go against Chuck's judgment. He knew the industry and, even more importantly, the pitfalls I couldn't foresee at that point in my career.

"What if," I said tactfully over a plate of fried chicken and mashed potatoes at Denny's, "we just . . . gathered some facts from the seller."

"No."

"Chuck, a little recon would give us insight into the possibility of a buy-out. It doesn't mean we'd have to move forward with an offer. I'm just curious, is all."

"No," he repeated. "It's a waste of time."

Chuck was headstrong, but I was equally as stubborn when ideas sparked my imagination.

"Chuck," I said, "we have nothing to lose by getting some information! We have no idea how much they're willing to sell for, and what assets might be included in the deal. It's worth it, even as just competitive research, you know?"

He pushed the last bite of food in his mouth and stared at me.

"Fine. But you're doing all the work."

The next day, I contacted the president of the company and asked some general questions. Then, we booked a flight to Cleveland for a meeting. The info was pretty favorable; I pushed Chuck to continue pursuing this potential prey. We wanted to check out their facility in Atlanta and assets to determine the value for ATCO, and they agreed on one condition: that we put down $50,000 in earnest money to see their production, offices, and warehouse. If, after our tour, we decided to not move forward with the deal, we'd forgo that money. But, if we proceeded and acquired the company, it would be applied to the sale price.

I thought this a prudent and reasonable ask since we were their fiercest competitor in the market, and they didn't want to give away any of their secrets to us for free. But Chuck, like clockwork, balked. "No," he said, "I refuse to give them money up front. It's not fair."

"What have we got to lose?" I asked.

"Fifty thousand dollars is what!" he yelled.

"But look at the knowledge we'll gain about their machinery, their technology, their workflows. We'll get insight into how they compete with us, and in what areas they're winning. The risk/reward ratio is in our favor. Trust me. This is a risk we should take."

After a while, Chuck agreed, saying, "Fine. But you must pay for this out of your own pocket," and laughed at the surprise in my face.

I was so sure of this acquisition, I contacted my bank, sent the wire, and arranged for Chuck and me to visit their facility in Atlanta and meet the factory workers there. Walking in, I was shocked; the equipment was brand new, well laid out, running efficiently, and operated by a trained workforce. Not only was their setup better than I expected, it was better that ATCO's! Chats with supervisors and production workers further solidified my vision of their dedication. On the plane back to Dallas, Chuck agreed; we should move forward with an offer. We discussed how to combine our operations with the one in Atlanta and listed the benefits of such a move. Chuck put me in charge of future plans and gave me full authority to head the transition.

There was still one problem; we didn't have the money to buy them out.

"Let's talk to the bank, just in case," I told Chuck. Our bankers were effusive with their confidence in us and lent us the money right away. We then made a plan: to conserve cash and make ATCO as solvent as possible before going ahead with the acquisition. Within a month, we had improved liquidity and needed to borrow less than we expected.

Our return trip to Cleveland brought us all to the table to close. We checked the finer details of the company and gave our final offer. We looked at sales, customer base, supplier lists, and assets versus liabilities. Suddenly, Chuck was furious. Included in the fine print, the seller added a leased building, which they'd failed to mention in their original offer. This building raised our price by $50,000, to which we had to agree to close the deal. Fuming, Chuck thought it a shady tactic to gouge us for more money than we'd negotiated. "No," I said, and our lawyer agreed, "this was an honest mistake. Don't let this little snafu get in the way of such great potential for ATCO. They're not trying to cheat us, and we can afford it. Let it go."

Chuck still wanted to walk away. I insisted, "If you care about the future of ATCO, we have to buy this company."

"Fine!" Chuck yelled, throwing down his pen. "But this is your baby. You're responsible for what happens." In other words, my neck was on the line.

———◆———

Chapter 26

❧

It *was probably the fact* that Chuck put the weight of ATCO's success on my shoulders that I began working twelve-hour days. After we signed the paperwork, we had a lot on our plate—or, rather, *my* plate. I was to manage merging our new acquisition into the ATCO fold, which included a new factory in Grand Prairie, which was located smack dab between Dallas and Fort Worth. Every day, I'd drive between these cities and up to our headquarters north of Fort Worth, clocking hours and miles that kept me away from my family. We also acquired a factory in Atlanta, and I was on a bi-monthly schedule flying there to coordinate their activity and optimize production.

> **CALCULATED RISK #4:**
>
> Acquiring a competitor company against my boss's wishes with the hopes of national expansion.

ATCO was inching toward becoming a national company, and as I integrated our new buildings and staff and capabilities, I realized we needed a dedicated marketing director to create ads on a national level. This person would work directly under Chuck. For four months, we interviewed candidates, but Chuck wasn't satisfied. One morning, Chuck started to laugh.

"What's so funny?" I asked, slightly annoyed. I had a stack of to-dos on my desk, and we were still stuck on filling this position. I was exhausted.

"I just realized we already know the best person for this job. They've been under our nose this whole time; I just wasn't paying attention."

"Who?" I asked.

"You!"

"Oh no, sir. I have zero experience in sales and marketing."

"Don't be humble, Ramesh. It doesn't look good on you." I was taken aback.

"No, really . . ."

"Ramesh, I saw you step up when K. left ATCO. I've seen your work. You can do this. And, you must do this. I won't take no for an answer."

I was flattered but hesitant. More work and longer to-do lists weren't going to help me see my family more often. Anita and Niraj were growing up fast, and I was constantly missing karate meets and soccer games. I worried about what Kalpana would think with another load of work added to my pile. But I knew Chuck was right. I didn't really have a choice. That day, Chuck made the announcement of filling the position to our entire staff.

I found myself in a dilemma. How could I market ATCO so that it would become a brand leader in flexible ducting? Competition was fierce. So many companies lowered their prices or offered deals to lure customers their way. I didn't want to cut into our profits—we had to make money, and the more money we made, the better positioned we'd be to acquire more companies. My long-term goal was ambitious: To become a global brand leader, we had to conquer the United States first, which meant factories across the country to connect our products to contractors as quickly and reliably as possible.

I sat down one day to look at market demand. ATCO manufactured ducts, then shipped to a wholesaler, who then sold to a contractor. I decided to focus all my energy on the contractor's experience because they, not the wholesaler, were our end customer. And contractors worked like this: When it comes to installing flexible ducts in a new condo complex or airport, all is well in dry, sunny weather. But when it rains, the contractor can't install anything. Bad weather can push back an install for days, but once the storm passes, contractors scramble to get the ducts installed ASAP. They'll buy whatever the wholesaler has in stock. In other words, they worked on a twenty-four-hour timeframe to purchase ducting from our wholesalers.

That's when it hit me. To compete against rival brands, we didn't have to lower our prices and potentially cut into our profits. Instead, we could make sure ATCO products were always available so that on that first sunny day, contractors could immediately purchase and install our ducts. To make sure ATCO was on the shelves, we'd have to speed up delivery time.

Now, the industry standard was seven to ten days for delivery. Most ducting companies lacked a sophisticated distribution system, and they struggled to make deliveries even in that timeframe. Distributors would stockpile goods that would then get depleted after a bout of nasty weather, and many contractors would be left empty-handed on a beautiful day and get berated by their client for wasting precious time on their building.

So, my job was to disrupt this clunky system and make sure every contractor in the company equated ATCO with reliability *and* availability.

This is when I implemented the second major change at ATCO that influenced our industry forever.

I came up with a little idea called "Quick Delivery." I decided what would make ATCO a star in the industry was to make a bold claim—and follow through on that claim. ATCO would promise to deliver product to a distributor in three days or fewer. That way, distributors could promise contractors that ATCO products would always be in stock. And, if the product wasn't in stock, ATCO would get product to them in three days or fewer, undercutting our competition by a week. And, if a contractor had their own truck, we'd promise they could call in an order and pick it up from our factory the next day. With that edge, nobody could match ATCO. And we could keep our prices high and customers would pay a premium for dependability because it would keep their clients happy.

"Jesus, Ramesh. This is too audacious, even for you."

"I believe we can pull this off, Chuck!"

"We've been delivering our products the same way for twenty years. There's no reason to switch that up now. And besides, everyone else in the industry delivers on these timetables. It's too much of a risk."

"Remember when we changed our invoice system, and it revolutionized our product flow? You thought that was a risk too. And look how well it paid off."

"This is different!" he roared. "This is promising our customers the impossible! It'll backfire. We won't be able to deliver, and ATCO's reputation will be ruined!"

"Don't you trust me yet, Chuck, after all these years?"

Chuck sighed. "Honestly," he said, "I think it's impossible. Promised delivery in three days?"

"I promise you, Chuck. I can do it."

"Fine!" he huffed, without an ounce of faith in his voice. "You always do what you want to do anyway."

I quickly got to work. I knew, to implement "Quick Delivery" adequately, I needed three things. The first was organizational; we needed a computerized system to integrate our new initiative. I told our IT director, J. D. Ratland, to build out a system that would track our manufacturing and shipping capabilities across all our factories in different states for timely deliveries. The second was practical; we had five plants and needed more. I knew that to make "Quick Delivery" work, we'd need shipping locations within a day's drive of the majority of our customers across the country. I analyzed sales, traveled the country, and assessed the risk involved in acquiring more factories. J. D. promised me that with his new computer program in place, ATCO could easily scale up to ninety-nine factories, if we wanted to. Of course, we didn't need that many. But, at the very least, we needed to double the number of plants we already had. I started scouting for sites to acquire or build out so that we would have a manufacturing plant no more than five hundred miles from most of our customer base. I drew circles around areas that lacked a plant and set out to acquire small competitors in those designated geographical locations.

You see, acquiring a competitor was so much better than building a brand-new plant. Buying a company gave us an established customer base and production capacity, which ATCO could then tap into immediately. I soon swallowed up companies in Baltimore, Maryland; Indianapolis, Indiana; and Vineland, New Jersey. I also purchased buildings in Riverside, California and Houston, Texas as well as one in Mississippi. By the end of my shopping spree, ATCO ran thirteen shipping facilities. The last nail in our marketing sweep was transportation; we needed our own fleet of trucks to ship product on our timetable to maintain reliable deliveries. We then purchased company-owned trucks, complete with "ATCO" written in large letters along their sides, to service customer and distributor orders as rapidly as possible.

With a "Do not disturb" sign on my office door, J. D. and I worked together to streamline our new distribution model. If we loaded trucks on Monday or Tuesday evening for a Thursday/Friday arrival, all our plants would have the supplies they needed to meet delivery targets the next week. We drew out our supply chain with pencils on computer paper and located any flaws in the flow of supplies, goods, and finished products. We kept our system under lock and key, and to this day, nobody knows how it works besides ATCO's IT department and me. I realized, while creating this proprietary system, that it held our edge in the industry. I saw that the more secrets we could keep inside our walls, the more impossible it would be for competitors to scoop our customers.

Our "Quick Delivery" system worked like a charm! Everywhere we opened a new warehouse, our sales doubled. Our sales grew from less than 20 million to 300 million. Sure, to meet our three-day delivery guarantee, we incurred higher freight costs, but with such a high standard of reliability, our customers were happy to pay a premium for our products. In many areas, ATCO controlled more than 70 percent of the market. We sometimes had to refuse new customers because we were oversaturated with business. The competitors that were still around couldn't deliver like ATCO, and often, their only choice to retain business was to cut prices—which for them was at a loss, while we never had to lower our prices a cent.

Even with air-tight logistics and quick delivery, I knew this entire system wouldn't work without happy employees. I made sure our truck drivers made great wages and minimized the number of nights they'd have to sleep away from home. I drew delivery lines to prioritize short trips. Feeling supported, our drivers had time and energy to become friends with local customers, who, in turn, felt like they were receiving preferential treatment. Our drivers would come back to ATCO full of stories about the daily concerns of our customers, how competitors were faring, and the health of small businesses across the country.

As our "Quick Delivery" system—years before Amazon enacted a similar ethos, I must say—made our profits grow quarter over quarter, ATCO soared over the industry. Our customers were eager to work with our drivers and salespeople. Folks who wanted to pay the lowest price for ducting began to see the advantage of buying from ATCO—at a higher price, but with the advantage of a strong relationship, of feeling heard, of mattering. Our products were 5 to 10 percent more expensive than our competitors, but people paid that premium price tag because our service was flawless.

Business is all about building a relationship with your customer base. The foundation is trust, the walls are quality products, and the roof is service.

Now that we had the foundation and roof, let's talk about the walls.

Why were ATCO ducts so in demand? Why could we sell at such a premium and keep our profits rising? The answer is in the quality control of our ducts. We wanted to produce the best quality product on the market, and we wouldn't cut any corners for profit. For example, our ducts were made with wires that had to have a certain thickness and metallurgical quality. Our suppliers would moan "You're too picky" when we would reject anything that failed to meet our standards. "Yes," I would reply, "we are picky. Picky enough." Customers would even ask us to lower our prices, which we refused. "Just use cheaper wires," they'd say. "No," I replied, "I'll take many risks, but one risk I won't take is cheapening our product. We're giving you the best in the world."

Most customers respected us for that. We used the best flame-retardant materials. We were one of the first companies to use UV-resistant materials. We even developed a way to produce our own wires. I remember the day the machines arrived, and I watched in awe as these huge rods of steel were fed in and wire would come out. Nobody could believe we started making our own wire. It made us even more independent; it sped up production, and we sold our excess wire to competitors. Soon, we could dictate wire prices in the industry. This was how strict I was with keeping ATCO ducting the best product on the market.

To broadcast our quality to our customer base, we sought out approval ratings from agencies such as the Underwriters Laboratories. At one point, a customer complaint came to my desk, asking me to save him some money by dropping the UL label, but I insisted quality control was too important to let slide.

I also implemented two more layers of secrecy in our company. The first was our machinery, which we designed and manufactured ourselves. I refused to buy machines available on the open market, and I refused to patent ATCO machines. You see, when you take out a patent in the United States, it expires in twenty years. After the expiration date, your technology automatically enters public domain, and anyone can copy it. With no patent, we never had to make our designs public. I kept a tight grip on our proprietary technologies; I wouldn't let anyone tour our factories. Once, Chuck had to call me to convince a factory manager to let him and his wife into a plant. Our policy was that strict.

The second was our adhesive recipe used to coat our flexible ducting for flame retardancy. It was a secret blend of ingredients that no one knew except for me and our head of R&D. We would purchase ingredients from thirteen different factory suppliers. These supplies would be shipped to ATCO's plants in different locations. They were then tasked to make batches of chemical mixes with the chemicals they received. Each batch was called either Masterbatch A or Masterbatch B. Both batches would be sent to plants with a recipe calling for different percentages of Batch A and Batch B to make Masterbatch C. This final batch would be used in the final product. The formula was kept hush-hush to prevent even our own employees from knowing how to make it. Our plant workers would receive A and B, never C. Sure, we could have mixed the final glue product in Fort Worth and sent it out, but this way, our knowledge was protected along the entire manufacturing chain. This high-level secrecy prevented competitors from being able to copy us, and it insulated ATCO into creating a product that was durable and unique all over the world. Our edge, I knew, lay in secret knowledge.

This rule helped ATCO dominate international markets. There was an "aura" in the market that we had a "magic" formula that made our products special. This "aura" did a lot to make our products more in demand than they otherwise would have been. Because of this, we had a huge R&D department—bigger than most other companies in our field. And I kept that department close to my vest because I knew it was one of the major ingredients of our success.

By the end of the 1980s, ATCO controlled most of the market, which meant we got to control the price of ducting. We'd see competitors adjusting their prices based on ours. Trying to keep up, they attempted to copy our delivery system and our supply chain management, but they could never match us. Some would lose enough money that they'd throw in the towel, which usually meant they'd call us with an offer to sell. We bought several small companies that way through the decade, and with each acquisition, our market share increased.

ATCO became known as the American Kings of Flexible Ducting.

———•———

Chapter 27

I*t was ironic that I left* Frederick R. Harris to work for ATCO to settle down and give stability to my family, when in fact ATCO had me traveling all over the country, missing important milestones in my children's lives. I would tell myself, "At least I didn't have to move Kalpana and my kids from country to country." But even then, I spent so much time away from them. These moments away from them added up to a chunk of time I can never get back. But it was a sacrifice I had to make, and I knew if they didn't understand then, they would one day. And I would make sure, as Anita and Niraj got older, they would be taken care of, just as I was taking care of them then . . . even though it may not have felt like it, since I was on the road or in the air all the time.

All of this hard work and travel paid off in 1992 when I was able to buy ATCO outright from Chuck over a five-year period with very favorable terms. My goal was to make Chuck very prosperous while also securing the opportunity to run the company exactly how I wanted. We worked well together for the rest of our business lives, and in 1994, at fifty years old, I became the President and CEO of ATCO Rubber Products.

———•———

Chapter 28

~

B*y the time I became the sole owner* of the business, ATCO had overtaken the U.S. market, dominating the industry from coast to coast. During the prior decade, we scaled our company larger than Chuck had ever imagined, controlled the price of our products, and kept our employees and customers happy. Kalpana was proud of me—even with the large hole I left with my constant traveling—and she urged me to slow down, enjoy the success I'd brought to ATCO, and spend more time at home.

But I wasn't done with ATCO quite yet. I knew we could expand further—yes, we had the United States, but my goal was still the world.

Enter Harendra—my wily, enthusiastic, and entrepreneurial brother, who we last left in the outskirts of New York City all those years ago. As I moved my family to Michigan and then Texas and built out a ducting kingdom, Harendra found success as an international salesman. Through the '80s, he spent his time on the road too, traveling throughout Europe and meeting with prospective clients. Every time he took a trip, he ended up with a slew of new German, French, and Italian friends.

During his travels, Harendra met a businessman in Australia who wanted to add ATCO ducting to his product line. He owned a company outside of Sydney that manufactured fiberglass insulation. He approached me with an interest in ATCO selling him the inner core and jacket of our ducting, which he could use to assemble a finished product. Chuck and I met him in Dallas to talk it out, and after a few days, we reached a deal to sell him the components he wanted. The testing and approval process took forever, but I was able to travel to Sydney during this time to train their workers. Once we got the green light, this company manufactured flexible ducting using ATCO components and distributed them across Australia and New Zealand. Within a year, we were the largest flexible duct manufacturer and distributor in that region of the globe.

Although our time in Australia was short (the owner of the company was bought out by a large New Zealand conglomerate that dropped ATCO as a supplier after a few years), it opened my eyes to what was possible overseas. Now, I had the green light to expand even further.

One evening in 1997, Harendra and I ate dinner at a local restaurant in Dallas. As we caught up with each other's lives and businesses over a few beers, I told Harendra that I had an itch I wanted to scratch, but Chuck, in his consulting role at ATCO, was being stubborn and told me it was a terrible idea.

"What is the idea?" Harendra asked.

"I want to bring ATCO to the international market. I'm sure we could conquer the world just as we have the United States. Chuck was adamant. He is against selling to foreigners."

"What?" my brother said, a bit shocked. "Why?"

I lowered my voice. "He doesn't trust them. He says they never pay on time. He's afraid they'll take our money and run."

Harendra sat in thought. "You know," he began, "I already have tons of relationships with buyers in Europe. What if I add ATCO to my product list? I just opened a new distribution warehouse in Dubai."

"That's brilliant! Then, I can prove to Chuck that we can make money in a foreign market." We clanked pint glasses, and the next day brought the idea to Chuck.

"Okay," he said begrudgingly. "It's your company, you know. But just make sure you get paid."

Soon, I began shipping ATCO materials to the Dubai warehouse, where Harendra would assemble and sell our products under our brand name. ATCO's reputation spread overseas, and my brother was met with excitement when prospective buyers found out our products were now available to them. Without much effort, ATCO was now available to customers in Saudi Arabia, Bahrain, Kuwait, and other countries in the Middle East. Sales continued to rise. But there was one snag; to sell in Europe, we had to get local code approval, which required extensive testing. Investing in such testing was cost-prohibitive at that time. I knew we needed a plant in Europe; ideally, something that already existed and already had code approval. We needed an acquisition.

———◆———

Chapter 29

~

That *same year, I attended a trade show* in Frankfurt, Germany with Harendra. My brother told me a handful of manufacturers in Europe wanted to join forces with ATCO in a joint venture to become the dominant supplier of flexible ducting in Europe. A small company in Holland approached Harendra with the possibility; he refused.

The next year, I skipped the trade show because I had some business in India to attend to. While there, Harendra called me. "Ramesh, this company approached me again. They're begging to have a meeting with you. What do you want me to say? You could stop here on the way back to Dallas. At least talk to them—they're getting annoying!"

I was hesitant, but I agreed . . . on one condition. "I won't have a joint venture, Harendra. I'll do this for you, because I respect you, but I will either buy them out completely or walk away."

"Fine, fine, just get your ass over here!"

I flew into Frankfurt and Harendra immediately introduced me to the owners of the company. We chatted about their production, suppliers,

products, distribution system, customer base, and financial health. I
thanked them for their time, but even before I stood up from the table,
I knew I wasn't interested.

"Ramesh, please," Harendra pleaded. "Just visit their plant. Just be
open to the possibility. What have you got to lose?"

His words rang in my head and reminded me of how I used to speak
to Chuck a decade ago.

"Okay, fine," I said. "Set up a time when I can take a tour."

The owners were ecstatic. On the flight over, I made a list of pros and
cons regarding a deal with this company and decided to at least give them
a chance to wow me. I landed in Amsterdam, where a manager picked me
up and drove me to the factory. We wound through flat, marshy fields of
the Netherlands countryside until we entered a small village two hours
from the capital called Enschede. The factory was a small building on
the outskirts of town. And I mean, very small; they had about fifteen
workers and two supervisors. But, walking through their machinery,
I was struck by the quality of their equipment and the workers' ethos.
Without meaning to, I found myself imagining the changes I could make
to optimize operations here and turn them profitable. Two hours later, I
was convinced this was, in fact, a great move for ATCO. The only issue
in front of me was negotiating a price.

With a stack of financial statements in front of me, I leafed through
their history and current health report. The company was loaded with
debt owed to the bank as well as family members. Each quarter, they
were losing money without any sort of cash flow to support it. "They've
got three months to live," I realized. Then, my business mind clicked on:
"Which is leverage to make a great deal."

We met again and discussed the company's viability and liabilities.
The owners agreed on a price that I would pay in cash, which included

a decent salary for the two owners plus a percentage of profits. In the end, I couldn't say no. I would invest $1 million in the acquisition and own a majority share of the company; since ATCO's sales were over $200 million in the U.S., it was a small investment. But by my calculations, getting a foothold in Holland could *double* our annual sales—if we were successful. Low risk, high reward; this was a calculated risk I could handle.

Smiles flashed across their faces as we shook hands over the deal, giving ATCO majority share of their company. "There is no better feeling," one of them said, and I smiled. In my head I thought, "Yeah, you just offloaded a huge chunk of debt. You're welcome." We ended the evening at a pub with pints of Dutch beer. Tipsy and happy, I returned to my hotel room, certain this was a great deal I had just made.

But there was something else that didn't happen that's important to note; I hadn't consulted a lawyer or accountant or European consultant to guide me in my decision. I just went with my gut and bought the damn company. This was the fifth major risk I took in my life. With this acquisition, I entered a new market where ATCO had no presence. If this succeeded, we would have limitless potential. The company had all the licenses and approvals for products already, and ATCO could

CALCULATED RISK #5:
Acquired a foreign company on gut instinct to start our international expansion.

support them with our expertise in manufacturing and finances. Plus, the price they offered was quite attractive. I weighed that with the risk: worst-case scenario, the company goes bankrupt. Even if that happened, the effect on ATCO's finances was minimal. What did I have to lose?

Chapter 30

~

A*s the world entered the year 2000,* life was looking pretty good for the Bhatia clan. Anita was working at a great job, Niraj was studying business at USC, and Kalpana and I spent the weekends in peace and quiet. ATCO, meanwhile, had a firm foothold in Europe. I made it my top priority to optimize operations there and manage my personnel for maximum profit.

I overhauled their manufacturing system, rearranged their supply chain, and over the next two years improved their sales from $4 million to $10 million. I flew back and forth to Holland monthly to oversee the acquisition. All was fine and dandy, except for one thing. The two owners of the company fought constantly. Remember what I said about business being like a marriage? I felt like an only child caught in the middle of two squabbling parents, having to mediate their different opinions, calm their emotions, and give an ear to their grievances. After a few months, I couldn't take it anymore, so I talked one owner into taking an early retirement. The carrot I dangled in front of him was a bountiful severance package. But, always looking to solidify ATCO's place in the world market, I added a stipulation to his termination contract. ATCO would take full ownership of the company, and the remaining owner would stay on as a general manager with full operational responsibility of the company.

This cleared the cluttered air in Europe for me. It streamlined the chain of command. It was much easier for me as the owner to implement changes through one manager, and that allowed the ATCO branch in Holland to soar.

Four years later, another Dutch company called DKG approached me for a sale. I had a secret meeting with the owner in Schiphol Airport to discuss the details of a potential acquisition.

"I've run this company for a few years, and it's not doing well," he told me. "I'm interested in having a joint venture with ATCO. What do you think?"

"I don't do joint ventures," I said, firmly but warmly. "But I will buy you out. Here's why this is better for you in the long run . . ."

My new Dutch general manager objected to the deal and didn't want to proceed, but I saw the potential this company could provide, and I craved to build out our European market. Despite the GM's feelings, I bought the company in a secret meeting in Atlanta. (Mergers and acquisitions are always best to keep secret.) We signed a three-year agreement that gave me rights to handle all their sales and marketing and access their technology. We acquired their production units and gained $7 million in additional sales they used to have. Plus, we eliminated one of our major competitors in Europe.

Our sales in Holland went from $10 million to $15 million and gave ATCO economy of scale. That is, we began saving money by increasing our level of production in Holland. ATCO captured customers all over

Europe and Russia, Ukraine, Poland, the Czech Republic, and Hungary. I implemented the same Quick Delivery/high-price marketing model, which worked like a charm. ATCO became revered for our service and captured bigger shares of the market year over year.

At this point, I felt like I could buy any company I wanted in Europe. Over two and half decades in business, I prided myself on becoming a master dealmaker. I learned the art of calm. There is power in an easygoing attitude. Most business leaders run on adrenaline and high stakes, and often I'd be halfway through a deal when a CEO or GM would stand up, shaking with anger, and call the deal off.

"Hey," I'd say, "let's calm down. I'm going to go on a walk and relax in my hotel room. Let's get together tonight, no lawyers, just us, and have a glass of wine. We'll continue talking about it then." Most of the time, with some light banter and a bit of downtime to decompress, we'd end up agreeing on terms and shaking hands by the end of the night. My strategy was to always highlight the benefits for the seller. Both parties must walk away from a deal feeling like they've gained something. Both parties must be happy. If someone leaves the table feeling like they've been screwed, it's just not good business. With each potential acquisition, I stressed, "Look, you are number one. You need to make money from this sale. I'm not here to extract capital from you. You tell me what's reasonable, and we'll work around that."

And every time, it worked.

———•———

Chapter 31

∾

Well, *maybe not every time.* I had such a winning streak up until 2002 that I felt, in certain ways, invincible. As I celebrated twenty-five years at ATCO, I saw how my calculated risks had paid off—with the profits and quality products to prove it. Our reputation extended into countries I'd never visited. I heard stories about architects and engineers demanding ATCO products when working on large-scale projects. Our ducting was sourced to build airports, stadiums, mosques, and skyscrapers. Soon, like flowers attract bees, other competitors showed up in the Middle East and Europe to wrestle a piece of our business away from us, but they always failed. For example, ATCO held 90 percent of the Middle Eastern market, and no one could charge as much as we could for our products. I was well on my way to my goal of global dominance.

And yet, with all endeavors, there comes struggle, and the decade of '00 was full of them. The first had to do with Mexico. ATCO had several large customers in Mexico who constantly pressured us to open a plant there. They argued we would be able to serve them more expediently while gaining market share in the region. On top of that, with trade agreement in place at the time, we could export products from Mexico to other Latin American countries free of tariffs and duties. I did some research, looked at labor and building costs, and chose a small town near Monterrey in northern Mexico for a new plant. We bought some land and built a huge plant to take care of all our business south of the border.

This, however, proved more difficult than I'd imagined. The build took twice as long as anticipated; by the time we were operational, it was nearly impossible to hire qualified English-speaking managers to run the place. Our spreadsheets showed we would have to pay twice as much as anticipated to secure workers—more than our U.S.-based salaries, even—which made the financial viability of the place much less attractive. Still, we went ahead with the plant as planned.

But there were more woes. Labor and banking laws are strict in Mexico, which made it very difficult to operate there, and the new business our customers promised never materialized. Our factory ran below capacity, and although we kept trying different strategies to make the plant viable, after two years of operation, we admitted defeat and pulled out. We moved all our assets to the U.S. and sold the building to a U.S.-based clothing manufacturer, which also ended up being a money-losing venture.

This setback made me want to expand somewhere else, but where? ATCO had over a dozen plants in the U.S. and a solid hold in the Middle East. We had interested parties in Africa who asked us to expand operations there, but I was hesitant to transfer our technical knowledge and strategies to that market—I felt protective over our proprietary assets. I felt similarly about Asia. I insisted customers from those continents buy directly from our plants in the U.S. rather than open plants in their countries. The economies in Africa and Asia were just not attractive to me at the time.

However, my general manager in Holland begged us to move our operations to China. I was wary of doing business with a communist country, but I traveled there a few times to scope out the possibility. I never make a decision without evidence, even if I already know the answer before I do the research. My colleagues would say, "It's so cheap there, we have to look into it." On my visits, I felt a level of distrust. I knew, from talking with other CEOs, that Chinese companies had a penchant for stealing ideas, reverse engineering products, and selling inferior versions for pennies on the dollar.

After a few trips, I decided we wouldn't open a factory there. My team didn't understand. They looked at the potential profit margins and balked when I said no. "Look," I said, "we're being hit with Chinese competitors, but I won't go into China. I won't buy Chinese supplies." My general manager in Holland begged me, "We need to shut our factory here down and move to China. They're cheaper."

I looked at her and said, "Are we not smart enough to beat the Chinese?"

"No," she answered, flatly. "We can't beat China. It's just better there."

"I don't believe that. We can do better. When you give up, you give up. End of story. We're not giving up."

So, I turned my back on those regions and centered my sights, once again, on Europe. Our three companies were doing well in Holland, with one snag. Around that time, the European Union experienced a big tech boom. Wanting to become competitive with the U.S., they passed laws to make trade easier within the E.U., but as I watched and talked with colleagues in Holland, I saw that all the countries still hated each other. They were fragmented when it came to sales and purchasing, and more so than state rivalry in the U.S., countries in the E.U. put nation first when they went to the market. The French wanted to buy French; Germans wanted to buy German. Even though our production capabilities in Holland made it possible for us to sell to every customer in Europe, we couldn't sell to everyone.

France was a huge market, and I wanted to dip my toe inside its borders and have a French face to ATCO. One day, the owner of the largest manufacturer in France approached me. Over the phone, he told me about internal management problems in the company. The owner thought if he joined forces with us, he could utilize ATCO's expertise to solve those problems. I traveled to France to meet the owner and tour his facilities. The general manager was kind enough as he walked me through the details of their operation, but he had an air about him that came across as self-important. He would visit the U.S. and chat with me over California wines, which he loved. In Paris, he'd treat me to fancy dinners, and he had me over to his home to meet his wife and children. But he had a condescending attitude—mostly because I didn't speak French. Plus, I think he had a bruised ego from the possibility of a U.S. company buying his French one.

Things got personal. The goalposts kept changing as we negotiated a deal. Because of the personality clash, I decided to bring in an SPA firm to audit the company's records and advise him on whether to proceed or not. This deal was so big and potentially messy that I couldn't wing it like I did in Holland those years earlier.

After due diligence and many meetings, I decided it would be another good acquisition for ATCO and would finally get us into the French market. The senior managers agreed with my terms, and we decided to close the deal that Monday. On Friday, right before we were breaking for the weekend, the general manager put a new demand on the table.

"Look, Ramesh," he said with a smirk, "one of the buildings you're buying, I'm just not getting a fair price on. I hear there's a supermarket behind it who's looking to expand. I could get a better offer from them, so you need to raise your bid, or I'll sell it to them instead."

"This is ridiculous," I said. "It's based on hearsay! And what is this new demand at the eleventh hour? You're being unprofessional."

"Am I?" he countered. "I'm just here to protect myself. You know how business is."

I was furious. This wasn't like Clecon in Cleveland where the seller made an honest mistake. This was a last-minute price gouge. I stood up, walked out of the meeting, and paced around Paris for hours. I knew there wasn't a supermarket that would pay what I was willing to pay. The GM was just trying to needle a bit more money out of the deal, and there's nothing that angers me more than unnecessary greed. Plus, his smug attitude and flippant comments soured me on the deal. But I knew it would be a great asset to ATCO. I didn't know what to do.

I tossed and turned that night. I knew his demand was unreasonable. And how annoying that it was putting the entire deal in jeopardy. I'd already spent years on negotiations, and to walk away now would feel like a major defeat. Then again, I knew I shouldn't succumb to his demands just because of the time I'd spent on making the deal.

That Monday morning, two hours before our scheduled meeting to close the deal, I called my lawyer and told him the deal was off. I booked an early flight back to Fort Worth that morning and was on my way to the airport.

"I won't entertain any more options," I said. "I'm done with that company forever." My lawyer thought it a bold but prudent move, as did I.

Sitting on that plane, I was relieved. I had no regrets. And, looking back now, it was one of the best decisions I've ever made. It allowed me to focus on the existing parts of ATCO, holding my brand firm across the world. Sometimes, I learned, no matter how much you crave to expand, it's better to walk away from a deal than make a bad choice.

Back in Fort Worth, my senior managers were relieved, and business went back to normal. A few months later, I heard the GM ended up bankrupt. Poetic justice? Maybe. I just think it goes to show the importance of humility, no matter what you've achieved in the past. Once you let arrogance take over, business gets bitter. And nobody wants a bitter business partner.

———•———

Chapter 32

~

These *struggles aside*, ATCO was reaching peak operations. By 2005, ATCO made $300 million in sales and commanded a large portion of domestic and international markets. We were hired to supply ducting to U.S. embassies all over the world: the Ben Gurion Airport in Israel; the Dubai International Airport and the Burj Khalifa, the tallest building in the world; Heathrow Airport in London; the Queen Alia International Airport in Amman, Jordan; Indira Gandhi Airport in Delhi, India; the Murtala Muhammed Airport in Lagos, Nigeria; and many more. ATCO ducting was also installed in Olympic Games buildings in South Africa, Brazil, and London. ATCO became a trusted global brand. We were the Coca-Cola of flexible ducting.

An example of our brand loyalty happened during the construction of buildings for the London Olympics. At the last moment, the laborer ran short on a few sizes of ducting, and the contractor offered to install a similar product in its place. The architect and engineers refused. They demanded the original ATCO flexible duct. To appease them, the contractor chartered a plane to fly the duct from the U.S. to London to complete the product. Such was the power and reputation of ATCO around the world.

During this high point of success, I came home after a trip to Holland and found Kalpana introspective and quiet.

"I just got off the phone with Niraj," she said.

"How is he?" I asked.

"Good. Maybe too good. He's been living out in L.A. on the beach since he graduated from college, and I think it's time we offer him a job."

I thought about it for a few moments.

"Ask him to be a part of the company."

Now, it is traditional for immigrant business owners to bring their children into the company so that, one day, they would take over. But I never had that desire. I loved watching Anita and Niraj grow into the adults they wanted to be, not ones I forced them to be. Too often, I saw my friends' children become resentful of having to take on the dreams of their parents. I couldn't just put him in upper management. But Kalpana had a point—he was maybe having too much fun out there.

"I'll talk to him and see what he thinks," I said.

After a very spirited conversation with my son, he decided that working for ATCO would be a great opportunity.

"But," I told him, "no special treatment. You must get hired just like everybody else. Don't expect special treatment because you're a Bhatia."

He interviewed and got a job in the IT department, and we all decided it best that he move back in with us for the time being. A few weeks into the job, Niraj came home, visibly annoyed.

"Dad," he complained, "I'm not getting paid enough. My friends in L.A. are making $60–70K a year, and here I am, with a degree from USC, making fifteen dollars an hour!"

"What are you telling me for?" I said. "I'm not your boss—Paul Evans is. He's the one you need to discuss this with." Grumbling, Niraj understood. As teenagers, I told Anita and Niraj stories from when I was young back in India. They knew the story of my father bringing home British chocolates by heart. They both knew the family tagline; "Bhatias don't steal." This lesson, for Niraj, was just another version of that truth. My son talked to Paul Evans, and eventually he made his way through the ranks of the company. After a few months, he decided to work in finance instead, since he was always fascinated with economics, and worked there for years.

My nephew, Vikram, had also recently been hired by Harendra to help run production in Dubai. Niraj's first job in the finance department was to work with Vikram on transfer pricing of goods. The IRS wants U.S. companies to pay equal taxes on goods, whether they are sold domestically or internationally. I wasn't keen on figuring out the details of this system, and soon got audited by the IRS. I paid a small penalty, which I thought fair, and told Niraj to figure it out for me so it wouldn't happen again.

At the end of the fiscal year, I asked Niraj and Vikram to give me their financial report on Dubai operations. I was shocked to see they had turned that arm of the company from non-profitability to profitability.

"Wait," I said, "are these numbers correct? Did you make these up?"

"No, Dad," Niraj said. "These are audited numbers. They've been double-checked."

"You paid someone off, didn't you?" I teased, honestly thinking maybe they had. As they laughed and shook their heads, I was filled with pride. To thank Niraj and celebrate his good work, I took him to lunch at his favorite restaurant: Subway.

"Look, Son, I'm impressed by your work. You've really proved yourself—and the thousands of dollars I spent on your college degree. I want to give you a bonus."

Niraj's eyes lit up. I then pulled out an envelope and handed it to him. Opening it, he pulled out his bonus: a five-dollar Subway gift card. "That's for your hard work. Let it show that the work itself is bonus enough."

Now, used to my antics, he laughed. "Thanks, Dad," he said. "This is perfect."

———•———

Chapter 33

~

B*y the end of 2006, ATCO sailed along* as one of the most prosperous and profitable companies in the world. We had plenty of cash to spend on large capital projects. At times, our CFO would ask me where he could spend that money. Real estate was booming, and prices were going sky-high. The possibility of acquisitions wasn't there, so I told him to turn his sights on real estate. He decided to buy land and build a huge factory outside of Phoenix, Arizona to replace a small, aging facility we used in Riverside, California. This new plant would take care of our ever-expanding market in Arizona and service Southern California as well.

But we hit a snag after we started construction. We weren't zoned for the size of the building we wanted. Instead of getting mad, I told the CFO to abandon that site and find a new one, which he did, in Glendale, Arizona. There, we built an even larger factory, and with fourteen plants across the U.S., we kept up with the high demand for our products in the country.

We were rocking and rolling. In 2007, I began to get even more obsessed with our U.S. operations. One day, I saw a gap in our locations and wanted to fill it with another factory. The gap was in Albuquerque, New Mexico, and I found a building to lease. Over six months, we prepped it with our specifications and got it ready for production. Just as we turned the switch on and celebrated filling in our national footprint, the world got hit with the largest financial crisis I'd ever seen. I remember sitting in front of the TV that night watching workers from Lehman Brothers walking out of their office building carrying boxes of their belongings. The bankruptcy of that massive financial firm ripped through the world economy, torching everything in sight. Construction in the U.S. dropped by 50 percent. Business dried up. Contractors, distributors, and banks went under. Tons of companies were barely holding on and had to lay off hundreds of workers and shutter factories and plants.

ATCO was fortunate to have a large cash reserve. We weathered the storm in relative comfort. I watched as other, weaker companies went bankrupt. I knew ATCO could pounce and gobble up these competitors for a steal, but I didn't. Times were hard enough, and although we were "cash rich," we needed that capital to keep us afloat. In the end, we barely made it through.

Fortunately, I always operated along the philosophy of "don't rent, own" when it comes to real estate. On the books, ATCO's real estate portfolio was worth $80 million, so it was easy to use this as collateral to secure a large loan to improve our liquidity and allow normal operations during the crisis. My other philosophy also came into play: "Avoid major layoffs." We downsized production operations, reducing manpower commensurate with that downsizing, but we kept our old workforce intact.

With this infusion of cash, I directed my engineers to design the next generation of equipment that would reduce labor costs by 25 percent and improve the quality of the product. This idea ran against the beliefs of many managers at ATCO, but I insisted on investing money into our own research and development department.

In 2008, we were well prepped to take advantage of an increased volume of sales without an increase in labor costs. These machines we developed during the financial crisis indeed reduced costs and improved plant efficiency. We considered closing a couple of plants, but I vetoed the idea because it would compromise our core marketing strategy of Quick Delivery.

Chapter 34

~

As *business bounced back* and the financial crisis wavered in our rearview mirror, I had the insistent desire to expand again, that obsession with making ATCO bigger and better than ever before. But I couldn't find any U.S. companies willing to sell.

Back in Holland, there was a medium-sized competitor located about twenty miles from my factory called DEC (or Dutch Environment Corporation). DEC employed a hundred people and was a respected name in the field with a broad customer base. Through the grapevine, I heard they were in trouble. I knew acquiring this company would complement ATCO's business, so I contacted the owner, a man named Ton de Goeij, and held a secret meeting with him at a coffee shop in Paris.

"Your company is in trouble," I told Ton, "and I want to help by buying you out."

"Mr. Bhatia, we've made some wrong decisions," he told me. "But we're not looking to sell. We're doing okay. Honestly, we are."

"Okay," I said, waving my hand in the air. "That's great news. But let me talk you through what I can offer you, and then you can tell me to get lost."

I then did what any respectable businessman would do with a reluctant buyer: offer him a deal so delicious, he couldn't refuse.

I could tell Ton de Goeij was a brilliant man—he spoke four languages—but I knew, despite his words, that his company was in financial distress and needed an infusion of capital. I laid out plans for both our companies, showing him the immense benefit of selling. The icing on the cake was an offer of all the capital he needed to keep operating plus technical support from the U.S. For the cherry on top, I offered him the position of general manager with a great salary plus a percentage of profits. And finally, for the sprinkles on top of all that, I promised him that if I decided to sell the company in the future, I'd give him first right of refusal to buy the company at a discounted rate.

Unsurprisingly, Ton agreed. I had given him no choice. The deal saved him from imminent disaster and gave both of us a strong share of the European market. In good faith, I gave him complete freedom to do what he wanted—as long as performance met or exceeded profit objectives. Plus, I knew one of our weaknesses in Europe was that we didn't have a strong legal/financial manager of our operations there. Ton was brilliant at it, and so, in 2010, I made Ton the general manager of the company with full authority to make the combined company profitable and prosperous. ATCO grew by 70 percent in revenues, and 100 percent in profits within five years. Ton was a great worker, and his multilingual talents allowed him to connect with customers across Europe. Impressed by his swift success, I offered Ton a profit-sharing plan that motivated him even more in building the business into a continent-wide juggernaut.

The back and forth between Holland was taking its toll on me. I wasn't getting any younger. One night, I was writing emails to Ton at 4 a.m. I heard Niraj walking down the hallway.

"What are you doing up?" I asked him.

"I'm a night owl, Dad. I'm always up late."

Then it hit me: "I hate being up late. What am I doing, getting up at 3 a.m. to work on European time, when you can do it—and actually enjoy it?"

"Great point," Niraj said, and right then I decided to have him take over Holland operations. I got to sleep early, rose when I wanted to, and realigned my body with a sleep pattern that gave me back the life I'd missed for some time.

"Know your employees," I told Kalpana the next day. "And always work them for their strengths."

With Niraj working on Holland, I returned to the work I loved best: brainstorming innovative ways to bring efficiency to the ducting industry. I still felt there was room to grow. With helpful conversations with Niraj, I worked on a concept for duct fabrication that my colleague, Tom Harper, came up with. It was called "Cut to Length," and it was a production idea that only ATCO could pull off. Normally, a flexible ducting company sends their product compressed in a box with some components like a T or Y connector. These components get shipped to a contractor; then, a team of laborers pulls out the duct, stretches it to its full length, and cuts it to size. Tom Harper suggested we might ship in bigger containers with our product preassembled and cut to size.

This would be a major innovation for residential developers who utilize three or four unique floorplans that are then repeated in random order throughout the neighborhood. Since we would know the floorplans in advance—and thus exact measurements of ducting and connectors—contractors could order preassembled parts they needed per floorplan being built. This system would lower labor costs. Installation time would be cut in half. It would also cut down on construction site waste and save time and money during city inspections, since each joint assembled by a laborer must be inspected before it's approved to proceed. If the parts are preassembled, they're also preapproved. Many of the developments that used our products were residential, and I saw this system taking ATCO to new heights.

My colleagues, however, didn't agree with this idea—and sadly, to this day, it was never implemented. I lost money on researching this idea, but it didn't matter because I learned a lot. I still know it's a sound strategy, but my CFO and sales managers said no. They were looking at short-term impact and costs, and yes, it would cut into sales. This new system would also possibly make distributors redundant, since we would ship directly from factory to construction site. My vice president of sales was worried all our distributors would hate us. No one's heart was in it. So, in the end, I gave it up.

I still stand by this new system, though. Yes, it would lose money in the short term, but in the long term it would cut labor costs by 30 percent, it would cut down on waste, and it would disrupt the flexible ducting industry. But I understood the pushback and pressed it no further.

You win some, you lose some. But you always learn.

———•———

Chapter 35

∿

O*ne of my last major attempts* while owner of ATCO was to find any other route to expand. After some market research, I came across a U.S.-based company owned by a U.K. conglomerate that looked like an ideal candidate for acquisition. I flew to London and met with the management team. They were receptive, but hesitant. They asked for time to think it over and talk to their U.S. counterparts. Unfortunately, the head of that branch of the company rejected the idea outright. The U.K. conglomerate declined to entertain an offer. In confidence, I was told the U.S. manager didn't want to lose his job or work for me. That's why he refused.

A year later, the London team offered to meet again, but the results were just as disappointing. I had to realize, at that moment, that another acquisition wasn't in the cards. My march to global dominance was complete, and there wouldn't be any further drastic scaling of operations.

So, with the few years left of me running ATCO, I turned my attention to making our U.S. operations more efficient and nimbler. Of course, without scaling, our growth was now limited. I made small changes, but nothing could compare with acquiring companies that would double our sales and profits within a few years. Now, I could affect minor changes that brought 10- to 15-percent growth, and we now had to fight for every increment in sales growth.

As the housing market cooled, I lost interest in pushing ahead with acquiring real estate. ATCO was dominant; no one could touch our brand recognition or quality of product. Internally we were strong, and employees were satisfied just as much as customers were satisfied. At the height of our success, I could tell something was certain; ATCO was going to either stagnate or decrease in sales. Seeing this limited growth potential and feeling like expansion was a thing of the past, and after looking around the office and seeing an aging workforce, I made another big decision. I was finally getting excited about retirement, spending more time with my wife, and giving the employees who had worked with me for decades the chance to take advantage of what we'd achieved.

One night, after dinner with Niraj, we stood waiting at the valet stand for my car.

"You don't really want to run ATCO, do you?" I asked him.

He was taken aback. "Can I be honest?" he said.

"Of course," I replied.

"No. I don't."

"Good," I said. "That settles it."

I was honestly relieved. I had seen, many times, the way friends had put their children in charge of companies they had built. Many people want to keep the company in the family because they have a personal connection to it. But so many times, conflict arose between siblings about pay or position or power, and those conflicts swiftly moved from the conference table at the office to the dinner table at home. I wanted to avoid that at all costs.

So, I decided to call it quits as the president of ATCO. I was ready to sit at the other side of the negotiation table, one I wasn't used to at all. I was ready to sell.

Chapter 36

~

In *2016, I began prepping ATCO for sale.* As I gathered decades of financial records and met with my tax advisors, accountants, and lawyers, I realized I had not one but three separate entities. There was ATCO U.S., ATCO Europe, and ATCO Dubai. I looked at the laws of each country housing my plants, including labor, environmental, and cultural, and decided to split ATCO down those already solid lines. Once they sold, I'd split proceeds with my employees on very liberal terms.

I first met with Ton de Goeij in Holland to whom I had promised the first right of refusal. He was eager to buy the company from me, but he didn't have the money or means to secure a loan. I knew he was an excellent manager. He was capable, and his track record was impeccable. So, I decided to finance the transaction myself so he could become the sole owner of ATCO in Europe. We set terms so that he'd pay me back, in full, in seven years. The sale included a very lucrative real estate property, machinery, equipment, and an inventory of products in stock. I would remain available as a consultant as needed, but Ton would now direct all decision-making himself. With the ATCO brand, and materials supplied by ATCO in the U.S., Ton was set to continue his success in Europe. We signed in 2018 and celebrated over a bottle of champagne.

I then turned to Dubai. It was a small entity managed by my nephew, Vikram. There was no pressing reason to sell it, but our main customer expressed interest in taking it over. We had a few meetings, but they didn't go anywhere. After a while, I decided to keep Dubai under my control but also wrote up a contract to keep us in business. The contract stated that ATCO would continue to sell our products to him in an exclusive agreement to stay with us. Both sides agreed, and we kept ATCO in Dubai independent and under my control.

Now, it was time to focus on U.S. operations. My first goal was to make sure ATCO was at peak performance and had no liabilities that might hurt a sale. Business was good. Profitability was high. Outside advisors told me ATCO was a very attractive acquisition. "Your brand name, technical superiority, distribution system, and internal team make you a top contender in the industry," they wrote.

I could see decades of hard work paying off through those words. I had helped steer ATCO from a local Michigan company of forty employees to an international powerhouse that employed 1,200. I felt good and wanted to make the best deal; however, I still cared about ATCO, the people who worked there, and our reputation. I could have taken the company public and retired with partial ownership, but I decided not to. I didn't want to have any managerial role at the company anymore, irrespective of profit potential.

So, I decided to put the company up for sale to anyone in the world. The process took a few years. We first interviewed several advisors and chose one we had the most confidence in. This advisor would then go out into the world and find potential buyers. I gave our advisor a list of three necessary objectives when securing a buyer:

1. The buyer must be in the same industry; however, they could be located anywhere.
2. The buyer must have a similar work culture as ATCO. The bulk of my employees had been with me for thirty years. I didn't want anyone terminated because new ownership wanted to cut costs. I was willing to take a lower price if a company could prove they would treat my employees fairly.
3. I would offer my employees a healthy termination bonus so that, if they did want to leave, they felt respected and not just cast off for a quick sale.

The advisor we chose prepared a comprehensive book about ATCO. It included our history, sales growth, strengths, weaknesses, real estate portfolio, and other details. My team at ATCO reviewed the book and then sent our advisor out with it to a hundred potential buyers all around the world. As the months went by, we received many refusals. We also received interested parties who didn't fit my criteria, so we rejected them. Of the companies that seemed favorable and showed interest, we handpicked thirty companies to pursue. Our bank contacted them for financial information, and after initial meetings, I whittled this group down to ten candidates with financial strength, with a strong track record in the industry, and that showed a method of business that was similar to ours. Each of these companies had brand name recognition, quality products, and loyal employees.

I invited the owners of each of these companies to a face-to-face meeting for a Q&A. Then, I offered them an exclusive tour of our facilities in Fort Worth—which, as you now know, was a big deal. I showed each company our machinery, our factory process, and our delivery system. After ten days, I asked each company to make an offer with attached conditions for my review.

After a week, I received four firm offers. The other six declined due to various reasons, such as cost. I flew those top four candidates around the country, showing them each facility. Two declined to move forward, while two remained interested. However, I didn't really care for them all that much, so I decided to bide my time and kick the can down the road to see what might happen.

Meanwhile, a buyer in Tennessee who had originally declined earlier in the process approached me with renewed interest. I met secretly with the owner of the company. It was called Mueller, and within a few hours, we reached a tentative agreement. Over a few days, we put a contract in writing and began our due diligence. Mueller had a private jet, and they offered to fly our team to each of our factories to give them a general overview of ATCO's assets.

Mueller also interviewed ATCO employees, suppliers, and customers to make sure what I told them was accurate. They learned about great working conditions, fair treatment, and the strong relationships we'd built with customers and suppliers. Satisfied, they turned to internal matters. They checked our financial records, tax papers, labor disputes, environmental issues, etc.

I hired a law firm in Fort Worth to deal with logistics. The deal went through without a hitch, and I shook hands with the owner of Mueller on July 1, 2018. I was retained in a consulting capacity for a period. I looked back on the past forty years. Four decades earlier, I had taken a risk and joined a small company with no clear path to success. And now I sold that company, which I had come to own and led to global dominance, for a lump sum.

That night, I sat down with Kalpana and said cheers with glasses of champagne. A wave of satisfaction spread through me. I had started with nothing and built the biggest and best flexible duct company in the world. Nearly fifty years after I had moved to the United States, I had friends in every country and on every continent. I had traveled the world and become more successful than I'd ever imagined. A part of me couldn't believe it was ending.

One thing was certain; I wouldn't have ended up here without taking calculated risks. Many times, I put my entire life on the line to achieve what I believed could be done. Many times, I could have lost all my money, or my house, or my reputation as a businessman. But, as each risk came into view, I thought through each choice and calculated the repercussions of each. I always moved forward when the downside would be limited while the upside might be tremendous. Kalpana, my support, advisor, and best friend, reassured me that, even if a risk didn't pan out, we would find a way to survive. And, in each instance, not only did the risk work, it took us both to greater and greater heights of success.

Through this journey, I've always maintained the value of human dignity and respect. Nothing is more important than treating others with kindness. It's more important than money, more important than making the biggest deal of the century. If you respect the people you work with and act from your brain and your heart, you will never lose anything; you will only gain. I am a testament to that belief. I came to the U.S. with nothing but determination and a love of meeting people and getting to know them, and I found success when I put everything on the line.

Once my dream came true, I knew I wanted to give back—to those who had supported me throughout my life, and to those who, with a little help, could also make their dreams a reality. So, in 2010, my wife and I created the Ramesh and Kalpana Bhatia Family Foundation. We started small at first, giving out $50,000 to $100,000 grants. Kalpana reached out to two charities that help battered and abused women, and I began giving each year to my alma mater, the Bihar University of Engineering, back in India. Once I sold ATCO, we put the Foundation into overdrive, growing our grant size and constantly looking for nonprofits to help fund in Fort Worth and beyond.

For example, in 2014, the city of Irvine, in between Dallas and Fort Worth, was looking for funding to build a statue to Mahatma Gandhi in a local park. There are so many successful Indian men and women in this country—in Texas, especially—but none of them stepped up to help. It should have been easy to fund, but it wasn't. The community leaders reached out to me and said, "We still need $70,000, and we only get a few thousand dollars from each donor." I saw their anxiety and decided to give them a full $100,000 so they wouldn't have to stress anymore and could put their energy into the actual construction of the monument.

A few years later, my friend Tiffany Carson and I were having lunch. She was a banker, and we'd known each other for years. We were talking about charities, and she mentioned one called Communities in Schools. "It's tough to raise money," she complained. CIS is a program that hires counselors to look after a group of students in public school. These counselors are paid by the nonprofit to monitor the students' grades, check in on family life, and give advice about life decisions. The program is successful in supporting kids who have lost a parent or experience food unavailability. It's a program that is near to my heart, since I know how hard it is to grow up in a family without stable food sources, and one that has lost a provider parent at a young age.

"People have so much money," Tiffany continued, "but they don't want to give any of it away. Every year, we have to beg."

"Why every year?" I asked. "That's such a waste of time."

"You have to twist these rich folks' arms to get a dime out of them."

"Huh," I said. "What if someone just gave you a lump sum to cover all your costs? Enough so that you could invest and not have to fundraise every year?"

"That would be incredible and highly unlikely. It would be a big chunk of change."

"How much?" I asked.

She became thoughtful. "It would be a crazy number. Something like a million dollars."

I looked her in the eyes. "Okay," I said, "I'll give you a million."

Tiffany dropped her fork. Realizing I was serious, she ran around the table, hugged me, then called the president of CIS, sobbing with the news. It was the biggest donation they'd ever received.

I invited Anita and Niraj to attend the donation ceremony for CIS so the entire family could be present for the event. I have to admit, I was tired and wasn't feeling up to giving the keynote speech. Anita said, "Dad, let me do it," and walked up to the podium with such grace and poise that I immediately asked her to run the Foundation for the family. She agreed, and she's been in charge ever since. She's a natural leader and has done an impeccable job steering the Foundation. Niraj had been investing money in budding entrepreneurs and nonprofits for years on his own, and I asked him to join forces with the Foundation so we could all work together as a full-family affair. It's brought us together as adults and kept us close. Each of us has our own focus, but all decisions are made together. It's a beautiful thing.

One of my proudest moments with the Foundation happened in 2021. Kalpana and I needed some medical attention, and we went to the William P. Clements Jr. University Hospital at UT Southwestern. We were so impressed by the doctors, nurses, front-line workers, and staff who provided us with care. Also, we had seen how hard-hit medical workers were by COVID, and we wanted to give back. We heard the hospital was raising money to build a new tower to house a neuroscience department with brain-related specialties.

I thought about my legacy. I wanted my name on something permanent. Instead of making a minor donation, I said, "Why don't I fund an entire floor?" They agreed, and we gave them $5 million. With that level of funding, they named a section of the new tower after us: the Ramesh and Kalpana Bhatia Family Foundation Atrium. We also gave an additional $2 million to establish the Ramesh and Kalpana Bhatia Family Foundation Distinguished University Chair in Brain Science.

This is the kind of altruism I believe should be a common practice. I have a firm belief that everyone should give back to their community. The more money you have, the more you should give. I don't think philanthropy should be an obligation—it's just the right thing to do. These days, I see CEOs hoarding money. After a profitable year, they keep their workers at minimum wage while raising their own salaries by millions. It just doesn't feel right to me. For capitalism to work, those with the most should make sure those with less have a decent quality of life. It's very simple, and yet such a foreign concept to many wealthy businesspeople around the world.

At each step in my career, I never forgot the neighbors and friends who chipped in to pay for my ticket out of India. I never forgot the grinning face of Harendra as he sped around Patna collecting that money. I never forgot the grocers who gave my mother vegetables on credit so we could eat when she didn't have the money to pay for them. Each of these generous acts led me to where I am today; I wouldn't have been a success without them.

And so, as a manager and business owner, I made it a priority to help my employees as much as I could—to offer whatever I could to give them a helping hand in their own success.

For instance, I had an employee, years ago, who I heard was behind on her taxes. I brought her into my office and asked her about her financial situation. She was surprised I knew what was going on, but with a little prodding, she told me her situation. I offered her a low-interest loan so she could pay off her taxes and get out of debt.

Other times, I'd hear about employees who couldn't afford the down payment of a house, and so I'd again offer low-interest loans so they could secure a house and help them build equity. I bought a car for one employee who was coming to work late because of missing the bus.

I tell these stories not to inflate my own ego but to show what a CEO can do for his or her employees. Because I cared about my workers, because I listened to their problems and knew about their personal struggles, I was able to help them find footing and financial security and give them the stability everyone in this country wants to enjoy. Helping them didn't just ease their anxiety about paying bills—it also turned them into the best employees a boss could ever ask for. Most of the people who worked for ATCO never left until I did. I had employees who stayed with me for over thirty years. Yes, we offered competitive wages; yes, we offered generous perks. But the bottom line was that I respected them and knew that their success was the success of ATCO as well.

There was a time in the late '70s, early '80s when gas prices doubled in the U.S. Gas stations across the country rationed their supply, and you'd see long lines at the pumps. It caused a high level of stress for my workers, and I could tell they were suffering. I called a meeting. The faces in the room were glum. They were expecting bad news: layoffs, cut hours, ways in which the company had to save money in this recession by taking it out on the employees. Instead, I said, "I know times are tough. So, I must tell you, there will be no pay cuts for anybody—except me. I will take a cut and pay a certain fixed amount every month to our employees to defray the added cost of gas. Some of our employees drive long commutes to get here. They deserve a little break." The room was stunned. "Each employee can use the extra cash however they see fit. That's my gift to you until I see inflation calm down." The room burst into applause.

You see, I'm not greedy for myself—I'm greedy for my employees. I'm not starving or anxious about making payments on my monthly bills. If I spend thousands of dollars less a year, it's not going to kill me. This is what I don't understand about CEOs and presidents of companies these days. They make millions and then claim they need to cut back on employee wages and hiring. How much are they going to save? They never cut their own pay because they need the prestige, the company jet, the country club membership. That's bullshit. I hate the imbalance it's caused in this country.

All in all, I'm not unusual. A lot of Indians immigrated to the U.S. like me with nothing in their pocket, maybe just a college degree. Many of them had done incredible jobs in their fields. Some had family here to support them and put them on the right track. Others, like me, were the first of their clan to make their way across the world and start anew. I took that chance because I believed in a better future, for myself and my family. "What's the worst thing that could happen?" I'd ask myself. "That I'll lose everything? Well then," I would tell myself, "I'd go back to Patna. I'd find my way. There is always a way."

But I never had to go back—because I thought before I acted. I treated my peers with respect and I strived to leave smiling faces in every room I walked out of.

Now, in my seventies, I have three things I'm most proud of: ATCO products in major buildings around the world; my children, who are as altruistic as I am; and my Foundation, which I get to run with my wife and help those in need. This, more than the dollar sign in my bank account, is what shows me that I've made it.

Now, looking back, I want to tell that little kid in Hira Lal's dirt yard, running around like crazy, begging for a treat—we did it, Ramesh. We did it.

And we did it by taking calculated risks.

I think my father would be proud.

———•———

About the Author

Ramesh Bhatia is the retired President of ATCO Rubber Products, Inc. and founder and chairman of the Ramesh and Kalpana Bhatia Family Foundation.

"For years, I've been asked about the secret to my success in business. My memoir answers that question. It imparts valuable lessons to aspiring entrepreneurs, drawing from real-life experiences to showcase how strategic risk-taking can unlock a realm of opportunities for those with the courage to embrace it."

Ramesh Bhatia is a titan of industry. As a child in Patna, India, Ramesh saw rampant corruption in the business world. He vowed to leave his home country to make something of himself with dignity and respect. With support from his brother and friends, he immigrated to New York City in 1969 with only a mechanical engineering degree and $50 to his name. He quickly rose within the ranks of the consulting firm Frederick R. Harris to become a project-manager for complex oil and gas projects across the globe. Renowned for his talents and ingenuity, he was recruited by Atco Rubber Products in 1978. Never afraid to take calculated risks, he led the company's relocation from Michigan to Texas and grew the company from forty employees to nearly 1,500. As the CEO, Ramesh expanded Atco's reach to customers in over thirty-five countries. By innovating Atco's supply chain management, perfecting proprietary technology, and implementing a quick delivery network years before Amazon, Ramesh made Atco the gold standard of commercial ducting. Today, he and his wife dedicate their time to The Ramesh and Kalpana Bhatia Family Foundation, which they founded in 2006. The Foundation is dedicated to making an impactful change around the world, funding innovative solutions and programs that enrich communities and serve the common good. He currently lives in Irving, Texas, with his wife.